# GRACIOUS
## Gator Cooks

*Savor the Sunshine*

## THE JUNIOR LEAGUE OF GAINESVILLE

The Junior League of Gainesville, Florida, Inc. is an organization of women committed to promoting voluntarism and to improving the community through the effective action and leadership of trained volunteers. Its purpose is exclusively educational and charitable. It reaches out to women of all races, religions, or national origins who demonstrate an interest in, and commitment to voluntarism.

The Junior League of Gainesville, Florida, Inc. focuses on improving the quality of the lives of at-risk children from birth to five years of age living in Alachua County, Florida.

Information on obtaining additional copies of *Gracious Gator Cooks* may be found at the back of the book or by contacting:

Gracious Gator Cooks
The Junior League of Gainesville, Florida Inc.
P.O. Box 970
Gainesville, FL 32602
Fax: (352) 371-4994   Phone: (352) 376-3805

Printed in the USA by
**STARR ★ TOOF**
Quality Companies of Starr Printing Co. Inc.

COPYRIGHT © 1997
BY THE JUNIOR LEAGUE OF GAINESVILLE, FLORIDA, INC.
FIRST PRINTING
NOVEMBER, 1997 10,000 COPIES.

ISBN 0-9606616-3-8
LIBRARY OF CONGRESS
CATALOGUE CARD NUMBER 97-06 9786
ALL RIGHTS RESERVED

## Gracious Gator Cooks

In the tradition of *Culinary Crinkles* and *Gator Country Cooks*, comes the Junior League of Gainesville, Florida's newest collection of recipes. Get ready to fall in love with a delectable assortment of new delights like Carnitas with Salsa Asada, regional favorites like Red Snapper in Lobster Sauce, and local Junior League favorites like Cold Cream of Vidalia Onion Soup. Savor the sunshine of Florida with entertaining recipes—good for all sorts of sunny activities like picnics, barbecues and tailgating. Enjoy recipes from our Children's Choices section where young cooks will find recipes sure to appeal to their spirit of adventure!

Gainesville's charm is reflected throughout *Gracious Gator Cooks* with small tidbits of information about our community. As you thumb through this book, visit some of our community's most prized historic sites such as the Thomas Center and the Hippodrome Theatre, which are listed on the National Register of Historic Places.

The Association of Junior Leagues International has a rich heritage of projects serving community needs. Locally, we focus on children at-risk from birth to age five in the areas of health, counseling and education. As you read through this book, we will share some of our League projects, like the Guardian Ad Litem program, which have truly made a difference for everyone in our community, especially for our children. Proceeds from the sale of *Gracious Gator Cooks* will help initiate and support our many volunteer projects, as well as provide funding for mini-grants to community organizations.

Our recipes have been triple-tested for accuracy, consistency and taste. League and community members have donated their favorite recipes, representing a blend of traditional cooking and current trends.

Enjoy a few tales about our league from our beginning back in 1935 on "Aunt Carrie's Porch", which is featured on our front cover. You'll see just why "Gator Cooks" really are GRACIOUS!

## COOKBOOK COMMITTEE

| | |
|---|---|
| Co-chairmen | Wanda Denny |
| | Linda Sue Rucarean |
| | |
| Recipes and | Tracy Stubbs |
| Testing | Barbara Guyton |
| | Melinda McCoy |
| | |
| Editorial | Angie Bowdoin |
| | |
| Marketing | Garrett Bell |
| | Kimberly Brock |
| | Margie Deardourff |
| | Jean Gadd |
| | Mary Walsh |

The Cookbook Committee is indebted to League members, special friends and especially our families for their most gracious support and encouragement throughout this seemingly endless project.

## PROFESSIONAL CREDITS

Layout and Design, Art Direction and Photo Enhancements
· ComQuest™ Designs, Inc.
    Rebecca Burns
    Angela Saternus

Cover Concept and Design
·Santa Fe Community College; Dept. of Graphic Design
    Jayne Grant
    Mark Iglich

Photography
· Rebecca Burns—Front Cover
· Pat Horlick—
    - Century Tower University Auditorium (divider page 7)
    - Holy Trinity Episcopal Church (divider page 47)
    - The Hippodrome State Theatre (divider page 117)
    - The Thomas Center (divider page 145)
    - The Wilhelmina Johnson Center (divider page 197)

· Mark Iglich—Back Cover
    - The Matheson Historical Center (divider page 73)
    - Morningside Cracker Cabin (divider page 237)

· Alice Farkash
    - Gator Country Cooks Icon Design

# Table of Contents

 *Denotes a recipe from Gator Country Cooks.*

*Appetizers  &  Beverages*

## Century Tower and University Auditorium

On a walk across the historic University of Florida campus, you will discover Century Tower, a campus landmark. The 157-foot tower contains a world class 49-bell carillon which can be heard every 15 minutes.

Century Tower was built in 1953 in commemoration of the University's Centennial Anniversary. The Tower and the adjacent University Auditorium were dedicated to the University of Florida men who were killed in World War I and II. Built in the Gothic style, the Tower and Auditorium serve as a focal point for many of the campus activities such as lectures, concerts and conventions.

The original 1956 bell carillon, which was donated by the founders of Winn-Dixie, was replaced in 1979 with the precisely tuned bronze bell carillon now located in the tower. This bell carillon is one of the heaviest in the world at over 57,000 pounds.

The harmonious sounding of the bell from Century Tower brings back fond memories to University of Florida alumni who visit the campus. Not only is it a musical reminder of the University's endurance and commitment to higher education, but also a reminder of those who helped preserve our country's freedom.

THE PRECEDING PAGE PRESENTED BY ERIC W. SCOTT, MD
DBA FLORIDA NEUROSURGICAL ASSOCIATES

# APPETIZERS & BEVERAGES

### TUNA CAPER SPREAD

*10 to 12 servings*

2 6-ounce cans solid white albacore tuna in
   water, drained

1 8-ounce package reduced fat cream cheese

2 tablespoons olive oil

4 tablespoons fresh lemon juice

1/4 teaspoon Cayenne pepper

6 tablespoons capers, drained and chopped

4 tablespoons fresh parsley, chopped

1 teaspoon dried thyme

Combine tuna, cream cheese, olive oil, lemon
juice and Cayenne pepper in the bowl of
a food processor and process until
smooth. Transfer to serving bowl. Stir in
capers, parsley and thyme.

Serve as spread on French bread or party rye.

## Tofu Black Bean Salsa

*16 servings*

1 15-ounce can black beans

1 cup salsa

1/4 cup green onions, chopped

1/4 cup red bell pepper, chopped

1 tablespoon lime juice

1 tablespoon olive oil

1/2 teaspoon garlic, minced

1/4 teaspoon ground cumin

2 tablespoons fresh cilantro, chopped or
   1 teaspoon dried cilantro

1/2 pound firm tofu, diced

Rinse and drain the black beans and place in a large bowl. Add salsa, green onions, red bell pepper, lime juice, olive oil, garlic, cumin, cilantro and tofu. Mix well. Chill, covered for one hour.

Serve with tortilla chips.

## IT ALL STARTED WITH LUNCH...

*In 1935, Aunt Carrie (Mrs. James W. McCollum, later Mrs. J.H. Palmer) along with a few other young women, gathered together on Aunt Carrie's porch (pictured on the cover of this book) to talk about ways this group of women could make a difference in their community.*

*It was over lunch some 62 years ago that these pioneering women resolved to help fill the needs of Gainesville's impoverished children. They soon went to work in their kitchens to prepare and serve hot lunches to the indigent school children. Through the years, the School Lunch Program filled the stomachs of more than 1,100 children of our area with 176,000 hot meals. It was with this community project that the Junior Welfare League of Gainesville was born.*

*Today, although the School Lunch Program is now only a significant part of our history, the Junior League of Gainesville continues to find ways to improve the quality of life for the people of our community, especially the lives of our precious children. Proceeds for the sale of this cookbook will support the League's on-going efforts that benefit the area's children.*

In loving memory of Ruth Franklin Anderson, a member of the Junior League of Gainesville for 50 years.

KATY GRAVES

11

## ARTICHOKE TARTS
*Makes 30 small tarts*

1 8-ounce jar marinated artichoke hearts
    or artichokes in water

3 tablespoons mayonnaise

1 green onion, chopped fine

1/4 cup grated Parmesan cheese

30 small phyllo dough shells

butter, optional

Preheat oven to 375° F. Drain artichokes, reserving the liquid, and chop coarsely. Mix chopped artichokes, reserved liquid, mayonnaise, green onion and Parmesan cheese. Spoon mixture into each phyllo shell. Brush with butter if desired. Bake about 10 minutes. May be made ahead and frozen.

## BEER CHEESE SPREAD
*Makes 2 cups*

1 pound sharp Cheddar cheese, shredded

1 pound mild Cheddar cheese, shredded

1 6-ounce can tomato paste

1 teaspoon garlic powder

3 tablespoons Worcestershire sauce

1 1/2 cups beer

In food processor, add Cheddar cheeses, tomato paste, garlic powder, Worcestershire and slowly add beer last. Keep pulsing until smooth. Transfer into serving bowl and refrigerate. Serve with your favorite crackers. This spread ages well. Can be made a few days ahead of a party!

## TEQUILA-MARINATED SHRIMP

*10 to 12 servings*

3 tablespoons onion, chopped fine

4 cloves garlic, minced

1/4 cup olive oil

2 pounds medium fresh shrimp, peeled, deveined, leaving tails intact

1/3 cup tequila

1/3 cup lime juice

1/4 teaspoon salt

2 tablespoons cilantro, chopped

In a large skillet over medium heat, sauté onion and garlic in olive oil about 3 minutes, until tender. Add shrimp and tequila. Bring to a boil. Boil gently, uncovered, 3 to 5 minutes or until shrimp turn pink. Stir occasionally. Transfer shrimp mixture to a bowl. Add lime juice, salt and cilantro. Toss to mix. Cover and refrigerate 2 to 24 hours. Stir occasionally. Drain and serve.

### THE JUNIOR LEAGUE THRIFT SHOP

*The Junior League Thrift Shop is our primary source of fundraising.*

*Members of the community are able to shop for quality used household items, clothing and jewelry at affordable prices. Each year we hold an annual "Toy Sale" near the end of November. Donated toys are sold at low prices, making it easier for children of the community to receive toys for the holiday season.*

*Committee members, other League volunteers, and the Thrift Shop staff help make ours a highly successful Junior League Thrift Shop. Because of its success, we are able to channel monies back into the community. In 1996, for example, community groups received over $32,000 through mini-grants and three-year grants.*

*Although much has changed since 1935, when Gainesville's first "Salvage Shop" of the Junior Welfare League opened, one thing has remained constant: the Junior League of Gainesville's commitment to serving the educational and charitable needs of the children in our communities.*

AMERIPRINT

13

## ARTICHOKE BITES
*50 to 60 bites*

4 to 5 fresh garlic cloves, minced

6 tablespoons olive oil

1 14-ounce can unmarinated artichoke
hearts, drained and chopped fine

2 eggs, beaten

pinch of salt

6 tablespoons Italian-style bread crumbs

6 tablespoons grated fresh Parmesan cheese

The day ahead, sauté garlic in olive oil. Add artichoke hearts, eggs, salt, bread crumbs and Parmesan cheese. Stirring constantly, cook a few minutes until eggs are set. Refrigerate overnight.

Assembly:

1/2 cup Italian-style bread crumbs

1/2 cup fresh Parmesan cheese, grated

2 tablespoons fresh lemon juice

Preheat oven to 350° F. Combine Parmesan cheese and bread crumbs in bowl and set aside. Remove artichoke mixture from refrigerator and shape into 1/2 inch balls. Dip in lemon juice and roll in crumb and cheese mixture. Bake for 10 minutes. Serve warm or at room temperature. Serve plain or with a honey mustard or sweet-and-sour sauce if desired.

# King Size Steak Bites

*12 to 16 Bites*

seasoned meat tenderizer

3/4 pound round steak, 2-inches thick

1 clove garlic, crushed

1 cup red wine

1/2 cup butter or margarine, melted

1 tablespoon dry mustard

1/2 teaspoon garlic salt

1 teaspoon Worcestershire sauce

dash pepper

Few drops hot pepper sauce

2 hours before serving:

Meat Marinade:

Apply meat tenderizer to steak as label indicates. Mix garlic and red wine in pan, add steak. Place in refrigerator for 1 hour, turning once.

While the meat is marinating; mix butter, dry mustard, garlic salt, Worcestershire, 2 tablespoons meat marinade, pepper and hot sauce.

Heat the butter sauce slowly, reserving to pour over steak. Broil steak 3 inches from broiler 18 to 20 minutes or until medium rare turning once. Cut steak into bite-size strips, transfer to chafing dish, pour butter sauce over steak and serve with toothpicks.

### General Kirby-Smith's Punch

*Take about 1 gallon of strong green tea; put in a quart bottle of champagne, whiskey, brandy, a quart of claret, a little Jamaica rum. Sugar to taste. Add orange and lemon juice.*

### Green Tomato Jam

*1 1/2 pounds sugar*

*4 pounds green tomatoes*

*1/2 lemon*

*Make a syrup of sugar and a little water. Cut tomatoes and lemons in slices. Boil in syrup. Set aside until next day and cook to a jam consistency.*

### Hot Buttered Rum

*In a crock or wooden bucket, cover the bottom with about half an inch of hot water. Add a lump of butter about the size of a walnut, and maple sugar to taste, about 2 heaping tablespoons to a gallon. Fill the crock or bucket 1/3 full with good raw rum. Fill then to the top with hot water and another lump of butter and several sticks of cinnamon. Stir vigorously and serve the drink in crockery cups or wooden containers. Keep the container covered between servings. For an added punch use hot apple cider instead of hot water. This is a drink that will stay with you sometimes several days; consequently, it is not recommended for pink teas or cocktail parties. Try it after a duck shoot.*

*These recipes are from the Junior League of Gainesville's first cookbook*

**Culinary Crinkles.**

15

### FRENCH MUSHROOMS

*10 to 12 servings*

1 pound fresh mushrooms

1/4 cup butter

1/2 cup bread crumbs

1/2 cup blue cheese, crumbled

1 teaspoon dried basil, crushed

Remove stems from mushrooms and chop stems fine. Melt butter. Remove from heat. Add chopped mushroom stems, bread crumbs, blue cheese and basil. Mix well. Fill mushroom caps with the mixture. Broil 4 to 6 minutes.

Serve hot.

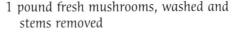

### EASY MUSHROOM APPETIZERS

*10 to 12 servings*

1 pound fresh mushrooms, washed and
  stems removed

2 to 3 tablespoons olive oil

3/4 cup pesto sauce

4-ounce wedge of Brie cheese

Preheat oven to broil. Brush inside of caps with olive oil. Fill each cap with 1 to 2 teaspoons pesto sauce. Top with small slice of Brie. Broil 2 to 3 minutes until slightly browned.

Serve hot.

## CHILE CHEESE SQUARES

*16 to 20 servings*

4 cups Cheddar cheese, shredded

4 eggs, beaten

1 teaspoon onion, minced fine

4 4-ounce cans green chilies, chopped

Preheat oven to 350° F. Combine all ingredients, mixing well. Spread mixture into an ungreased 8 x 12-inch pan. Bake for 30 minutes. Cut into 1-inch squares.

## BLUE CHEESE CRISPS

*3 dozen*

1/4 pound blue cheese, crumbled

1/3 cup butter, room temperature

1/8 teaspoon Cayenne pepper

2/3 cup flour

1/4 cup poppy seeds

Preheat oven to 350° F. Cream cheese and butter together until smooth. Mix Cayenne pepper and flour together, add cheese and blend well. Divide into two balls, wrap in plastic and chill 30 minutes. Roll each ball into a 1-inch thick roll and roll in poppy seeds. Cut in 1/4-inch slices and place on ungreased cookie sheet. Bake 15 minutes. Serve warm or at room temperature.

## BUFFALO WINGS
*4 to 8 servings*

1 pound chicken drumettes
1/4 cup hot pepper sauce
1 tablespoon Worcestershire sauce
2 teaspoons paprika
1/8 teaspoon Cayenne pepper

In a resealable plastic bag, combine drumettes, hot pepper sauce, Worcestershire sauce, 1 teaspoon paprika and Cayenne pepper. Seal bag and shake to coat chicken. Refrigerate and marinate for at least 30 minutes.

Preheat oven to 425° F. Remove drumettes from marinade and arrange in a single layer in shallow baking pan. Sprinkle with half teaspoon of paprika. Bake 10 minutes. Turn drumettes over and sprinkle with remaining paprika. Bake another 10 minutes or until meat is no longer pink near the bone. Serve with low fat blue cheese salad dressing and celery sticks.

## CRAB AND CAPER DIP
*16 to 20 servings*

2 cups onions, chopped

2 tablespoons margarine

2 cups mayonnaise

2 cups Swiss cheese, shredded

1 3 1/2-ounce jar capers, drained

1 6-ounce can fancy lump crabmeat

1 round loaf of bread

Preheat oven to 350° F. Sauté onions in butter until clear. Combine all ingredients, except for bread, mixing well. Cut top off bread and hollow out (save soft bread to eat dip with). Put dip in hollowed loaf and put top back on bread. Wrap in foil and bake for 1 hour. Do not double or half recipe.

## BLUE CHEESE SPREAD
*6 to 8 servings*

1 8-ounce package cream cheese, softened

1 3-ounce package blue cheese, crumbled

1/2 cup mayonnaise

1 1/2 teaspoons Worcestershire sauce

1 cup pecans, chopped

onion juice to taste

1 to 2 tablespoons milk (optional)

Cream the cheeses together. Add remaining ingredients. Thin with milk if necessary. Serve with crackers.

## "THAT JUNIOR LEAGUE PESTO MOLD"

*24 to 30 servings*

2 8-ounce packages cream cheese
1 pound unsalted butter, softened
1/4 cup pine nuts
2 to 3 garlic cloves
1 cup tightly packed fresh spinach
18-inch piece of cheesecloth
1 cup tightly packed fresh basil
1/2 cup fresh parsley
1/2 teaspoon salt
1/2 cup olive oil
3 cups Parmesan cheese
3 tablespoons butter, room temperature
fresh parsley for garnish

Beat cream cheese and 1 pound of butter together until smooth. Set aside. Roast pine nuts for 10 minutes at 325° F.

20

A CHORUS LINE FROM FOLLIES...

Prepare pesto according to sidebar directions or use 2 cups prepared pesto sauce.

## Assembly:

Moisten and wring cheesecloth. Line a 6-cup mold with the cheesecloth, smoothing any wrinkles. (A dome-shaped bowl works great and has a nice finished look.) Using a spatula, layer a quarter of cream cheese mixture then a quarter of the pesto mixture. Repeat layering process until both mixtures are used up. Fold cheesecloth over and pack down lightly. Chill at least 6 hours, or overnight for best results.

Unfold cheesecloth and flip bowl over on serving plate. Pull bowl up while holding cheesecloth down. (An extra set of hands helps.) Carefully remove cheesecloth. Garnish with fresh parsley. Serve with crackers.

This recipe can be varied by adding a layer of chopped sundried tomatoes to create a colorful and festive dish that is especially nice for the holidays.

## PESTO MAGIC

*Pesto is an extremely versatile sauce to keep on hand. Use this fresh taste as a spread for bread, spooned over chicken and fish or tossed with pasta. "That Junior League Pesto Mold" is pesto perfection for elegant entertaining.*

*1/4 cup pine nuts*

*2 to 3 garlic cloves*

*1 cup tightly packed fresh spinach*

*1 cup tightly packed fresh basil*

*1/2 cup fresh parsley*

*1/2 teaspoon salt*

*1/2 cup olive oil*

*3 cups Parmesan cheese*

*3 tablespoons butter, room temperature*

*Roast pine nuts for 10 minutes at 325° F. In food processor, puree nuts, garlic, spinach, basil, parsley and salt. Add olive oil and blend. Add Parmesan cheese and butter. (Do not over blend after adding cheese and butter.)*

JAMES MOORE
& CO., CPA'S

### COLD SHRIMP ROQUEFORT

*2 to 4 servings*

8 jumbo shrimp

2 ounces Roquefort cheese

1 1/2 ounces cream cheese

1/2 teaspoon green onions, chopped fine

1/2 teaspoon cognac or 1 1/2 teaspoons brandy

2 to 3 tablespoons fresh parsley, chopped

salt to taste

22

Steam shrimp until just pink, then shell and devein. Cut a deep slit down the back of each shrimp creating a pocket to hold the Roquefort mixture. Combine the Roquefort, cream cheese, green onions and cognac. Mix well. Stuff shrimp generously, then roll stuffed portion in chopped parsley. Salt to taste. Chill until ready to serve.

 *Idea!*

*Use a pastry bag or cookie press to fill shrimp neatly.*

## BLACK BEAN SALSA

*18 to 20 servings*

2 15-ounce cans black beans, rinsed and drained

1 1/4 cups fresh or frozen corn (use bagged frozen corn instead of boxed)

1 pound tomatoes, diced

1 bunch green onions, chopped (use only white and pale green parts)

1 green bell pepper, chopped fine

1 red bell pepper, chopped fine

1/4 cup olive oil

1/4 cup red wine vinegar

1/2 to 1 teaspoon Cayenne pepper

Mix ingredients in large bowl. Serve with tortilla chips.

 *Idea!*

*Use yellow, green, or red sweet peppers as attractive holders for dips. Just cut off the tops, remove the ribs and seed, and fill with your favorite dips for veggies or crackers.*

23

## GARBAGE DIP

*Makes 2 cups*

1 4-ounce can ripe chopped black olives

1 4-ounce can chopped green chilies

4 green onions, chopped fine

2 large tomatoes, chopped fine

4 ounces fresh mushrooms, chopped fine

1 teaspoon garlic salt

1 1/2 teaspoons salt

1/4 teaspoon pepper

3 tablespoons olive oil

1 1/2 tablespoons wine vinegar

Combine ingredients and refrigerate overnight. Serve with "scoop" style corn chips.

24

## Santa Fe Mini Cups

*Makes 24 to 30 mini-cups*

1-pound package wonton skins

16-ounce carton ricotta cheese

8 ounces jalapeno Monterey Jack cheese, shredded

8 ounces Cheddar cheese, shredded

1 4-ounce can green chilies, chopped

dash Cayenne pepper

black olive slices for garnish (optional)


Preheat oven to 350° F. Spray mini muffin pans with a nonstick spray. Using a biscuit cutter or glass edge, cut the wonton skins into circles. Place circles in mini muffin pans and lightly spray again with nonstick spray. Bake until brown (about 5 minutes). Mix cheeses, green chilies and Cayenne pepper, then spoon mixture into mini muffin pans. Place one slice of olive on top of each mini cup and bake for another 10 to 12 minutes until cheese is melted.

## PANINI
### (ITALIAN FOR ROLL OR BISCUIT)
*4 servings, or 16 to 24 appetizers*

1 loaf Italian bread
4 tablespoons extra virgin olive oil
1 cup Mozzarella cheese, shredded
1 recipe roasted tomatoes (see below)
1 cup whole fresh basil leaves, loosely
   packed
8 to 10 arugula leaves
8 slices Parmesan cheese, sliced thin

Preheat oven to 500° F. Slice bread in half
lengthwise; brush with oil and sprinkle with
Mozzarella cheese. Toast until cheese
melts. Top bread halves with tomatoes, basil
and arugula. Top with Parmesan cheese slices
and serve open-faced.

### Roasted Tomatoes:

8 large tomatoes
4 tablespoons kosher salt
3 tablespoons black pepper
1/4 cup sugar
2 tablespoons extra virgin olive oil
1 cup assorted herbs of your choice (parsley,
   rosemary, thyme, sage, basil, chervil, etc.)

Preheat oven to 250° F. Slice each tomato into
three thick slices. Mix salt, pepper and
sugar. Brush tomatoes with olive oil and
sprinkle with salt mixture and herbs. Roast
for 3 hours.

## PARTY HAM AND CHEESE BITES

*Makes 36 bites*

1 cup butter, softened

1 medium sweet onion, chopped

2 tablespoons Dijon mustard

3 tablespoons poppy seeds

1 teaspoon Worcestershire sauce

3 12-count packages of "party style" dinner rolls

1 pound smoked ham or turkey, shaved thin

2 cups Swiss cheese, shredded

Preheat oven to 350° F. Combine butter, onion, mustard, poppy seeds and Worcestershire sauce; mix well. Slice rolls in half lengthwise and spread butter mixture evenly on the inside of each half. Arrange ham or turkey on bottom halves of rolls and top with cheese. Replace tops on rolls and secure with wooden picks if desired. Place rolls on baking sheet and cover loosely with foil. Bake for 20 minutes and serve.

**Idea!**

*Slices of cheese cut with decorative cookie cutters offer a festive touch for special occasions. Try stars for the 4th of July, hearts for Valentine's Day, and pumpkins at Thanksgiving.*

## MARINATED CHEESE
*25 servings*

1 envelope Italian salad dressing mix

1/2 cup vegetable oil

1/4 cup white vinegar

2 tablespoons water

1 1/2 teaspoons sugar

8 ounces Monterey Jack cheese

8 ounces sharp Cheddar cheese

8 ounces cream cheese

1 4-ounce jar pimento, diced and drained

fresh parsley sprigs for garnish

Combine dressing mix, oil, vinegar, water and sugar in small jar. Cover tightly and shake vigorously to blend. Refrigerate to chill slightly. Cut Monterey Jack crosswise into 1/4-inch strips. Cut each strip in half to form 2 squares. Set aside. Cut Cheddar and cream cheese in the same manner. (Cream cheese is easier to slice if placed in the freezer for a short time.) Assemble cheese slices in rows like dominoes in a 2-quart dish, alternating Monterey Jack, cream and Cheddar cheeses side by side. Pour marinade over cheese. Cover and refrigerate overnight. Drain marinade off cheese. Arrange cheeses on a platter in 3 or 4 rows. Top each row with diced pimento. Garnish with parsley on the sides of the platter. Serve with crackers.

## JAPANESE EGGPLANT APPETIZER

*10 to 12 servings*

2 eggplants, peeled and cut into
  1 inch slices

vegetable or peanut oil for frying

2 tablespoons dark soy sauce

2 tablespoons sugar

2 garlic cloves, chopped coarse

1 to 2 teaspoons fresh ginger root, minced

2 teaspoons sesame oil (substitute hot
  chili oil for a spicier dish)

1 tablespoon cider vinegar

Fry eggplant slices in hot oil until brown and tender. Drain and cool while sauce is made. To make sauce, mix soy sauce, sugar, garlic, ginger and oil until sugar is dissolved. Set aside. Heat a little oil, add a little garlic and ginger and sear eggplant for 1 minute, turning rapidly. Pour sauce over eggplant and stir rapidly until sauce is absorbed. Splash vinegar around edges of pan to sizzle, stir eggplant. Pour into dish, cover and chill. Serve with crackers.

## CRAB DIP
*Makes 3 1/2 cups*

2 cups mayonnaise

4 tablespoons ketchup or chili sauce

2 teaspoons steak sauce

1 teaspoon salt

1/2 teaspoon curry powder

1 tablespoon Parmesan cheese, grated

1 pound lump crab meat
  (claw meat may be used)

Mix together and chill. Serve with crackers.

## SAUSAGE SNACKS
*60 pieces*

2 pounds hot sausage (pork, veal or turkey)

2 ounces chutney

2 cups sour cream

1 cup sherry (not cooking)

Preheat oven to 350° F. Roll sausage into 1-inch balls. Bake until brown, 20 to 25 minutes. Drain on paper towels.

Combine chutney, sour cream and sherry in sauce pan over medium heat. Stir in sausage balls to coat. Serve hot.

May be served out of a slow-cooker or chafing dish. Can be made ahead and frozen. Make sauce and combine just before serving.

## SHERRY CHEESE PATÉ

*8 servings*

2 3-ounce packages cream cheese, softened
1 cup sharp Cheddar cheese, shredded
4 tablespoons sherry
1/2 teaspoon curry powder
1/4 teaspoon salt
1 8-ounce jar mango chutney, chopped fine
3 green onions with tops, sliced thin
sesame or wheat wafers

Combine cream cheese, Cheddar cheese, sherry, curry powder and salt, beat until smooth. Spread on a serving platter, shaping a layer about 1/2 inch thick. Chill until firm. Just before serving, spread chutney over chilled mixture and sprinkle with green onions. Serve paté with wafers.

## FETA CHEESE IN OLIVE OIL

*24 to 32 servings*

3/4 cup olive oil
2 teaspoons cognac
3/4 teaspoon dried thyme
1/2 teaspoon coarsely ground pepper
1/2 pound Feta cheese, cut into 1/2-inch cubes

Combine olive oil, cognac, thyme and pepper in a jar and shake until mixed. Pour over Feta cheese and toss to coat. Cover and refrigerate at least 24 hours. Keeps up to one month.

Serve at room temperature with your favorite hot bread.

### CHICKEN-CHILE CHEESECAKE OLÉ

*12 to 16 servings*

1 1/3 cups tortilla chips, crushed fine
1/4 cup butter, melted
3 8-ounce packages cream cheese, softened
4 large eggs
1 teaspoon chili powder
1 teaspoon Worcestershire sauce
1/4 teaspoon salt
3 tablespoons green onion, minced
1 1/2 cups cooked chicken, shredded fine
2 4-ounce cans green chilies, chopped
1 1/2 cups Monterey Jack cheese, shredded
16 ounces sour cream
1 teaspoon seasoned salt
green onions, minced for garnish
Picanté sauce

Preheat oven to 350° F. Combine chips and butter and press on the bottom of a 10- inch springform pan.

Beat cream cheese with mixer until light and fluffy; add eggs, one at a time, beating well after each. Stir in chili powder, Worcestershire sauce, salt and green onion. Pour half of the mixture into the pan. Top with chicken, chilies and cheese. Carefully pour the remaining cream cheese mixture on top. Bake 10 minutes; reduce heat to 300° F and bake for 1 hour. Cool completely. Cover and chill for at least 8 hours. (May be frozen at this point.)

Just before serving, combine sour cream and seasoned salt, use this mixture to "ice" the cheesecake. Garnish with a rim of minced green onion and serve with Picanté sauce to be ladled over the cut wedges of cake.

## SHRIMP TOAST

*20 pieces*

1/2 pound peeled shrimp, uncooked and chopped fine

3 strips bacon, uncooked and chopped fine

5 water chestnuts, chopped fine

1 tablespoon green onion, chopped fine

1 tablespoon sherry or dry white wine

1 1/2 teaspoons salt

1/2 teaspoon sugar

1/8 teaspoon pepper

4 medium eggs, beaten

2 tablespoons cornstarch

10 pieces white bread, sliced thin with crusts removed

3 cups cooking oil

Combine shrimp, bacon, water chestnuts and green onion in bowl. Add wine, salt, sugar and pepper; mix well. Add eggs and cornstarch; mix well. Cut each slice of bread diagonally into two triangles. Place approximately 2 1/2 teaspoons shrimp paste on each slice, spreading evenly to the edges. Pour oil into large skillet and heat over medium heat. When oil is hot (350° F), place bread, shrimp side down, in oil until the edges are brown (about 1/2 to 1 minute). Turn to brown the other side. Drain well on paper towels and serve hot.

## KUO-TI
### (CHINESE POT STICKERS)
*Makes 40*

Filling:

2 cups water

3 cups Napa (Chinese cabbage), shredded

3/4 pound ground pork

1 tablespoon green onion, minced

3 tablespoons soy sauce

1 tablespoon dry sherry

1 1/2 teaspoons fresh ginger root, minced

1 package wonton wrappers

2 tablespoons oil

Sauce:

1/4 cup soy sauce

1/4 cup white wine vinegar

2 tablespoons fresh ginger root, minced

34

Bring water to boil in medium saucepan. Add cabbage, cover and cook several minutes until limp. Drain cabbage and mix with remaining ingredients to make filling. Place approximately 1 teaspoon of mixture in the center of a wonton wrapper, fold diagonally to make a small triangle. Seal edges by pinching, using a little water if necessary to get edges to stick together. Place folded side down on a flat surface so that the sealed edge is up.

Heat oil in a skillet. When hot, place pot stickers seam side up in skillet, almost touching. Cook about 3 to 4 minutes, or until bottoms are well-browned. Slowly pour 1/2 cup water into skillet, reduce heat to low, cover and steam 10 minutes. In small bowl, combine all sauce ingredients. Serve hot with sauce.

*Note:*
*These little treasures may be made ahead and reheated in the microwave.*

## Pesto Tortilla Snacks

*32 pieces*

1 1/2 cups fresh basil, trimmed and packed

2/3 cup Parmesan cheese, grated

1/4 cup pine nuts

1/4 teaspoon salt

1/4 teaspoon pepper

1/4 cup olive oil

4 10-inch flour tortillas

vegetable cooking spray

2 cups Mozzarella cheese, shredded

Preheat oven to 425° F. Blend basil, Parmesan cheese, pine nuts, salt and pepper in food processor or blender until smooth. With processor running, add oil by pouring a slow steady stream until combined. Place tortillas on a baking sheet coated with cooking spray. Spread pesto mixture evenly on tortillas. Sprinkle with cheese. Bake 8 minutes. Cut each tortilla into 8 wedges.

Serve hot.

MARCH 17, 1940

JR. LEAGUE FOLLIES
"HOORAY AMERICA" 1940

## Party Salmon
*20 to 24 servings*

4 6-ounce cans pink salmon, boneless,
   drain well
2 cups mayonnaise
3 dill pickles, chopped
2 medium onions, chopped
2 to 3 tablespoons lemon juice
1 black olive
paprika

Form salmon in shape of fish on platter.
Combine mayonnaise, pickles, onions and
lemon juice. Mix briefly in blender or food
processor. Cover salmon with sauce. Use black
olive for fish eye. Sprinkle with paprika and
serve with crackers

## Hot Taco Dip

*16 to 20 servings*

8 ounces cream cheese
1 can chili (with beans optional)
2 4-ounce cans green chilies
1 cup Monterey Jack cheese, shredded
   (jalapeno cheese, optional)
1 cup Cheddar cheese, shredded
1 4-ounce can sliced black olives

Preheat oven to 350° F. Layer ingredients in
order given in a 9 x 13-inch baking dish and
bake 20 to 30 minutes (cheese needs to
melt). Serve with tortilla chips.

## FROGMORE PICKLED SHRIMP

*8 servings*

1/4 cup pickling spices

piece of cheesecloth

2 1/2 pounds medium shrimp, peeled and deveined

2 cups onions, diced into 1/2-inch pieces

7 to 8 bay leaves

1/2 cup celery tops

Marinade:

1/2 cup vegetable oil

3/4 cup white wine vinegar

3 tablespoons capers with juice

2 teaspoons salt

a few drops of hot sauce

Whisk together marinade ingredients, set aside.

Tie pickling spices in cheesecloth, forming a bag and place in enough water to cover shrimp. Bring to a boil. Add shrimp and cook just until shrimp turn pink. Drain and set shrimp aside.

In shallow dish, alternate layers of shrimp, onion, bay leaves and celery tops. Cover with marinade. Marinate 24 hours or more, turning shrimp several times. Drain and serve.

## MUSHROOM AND ROASTED PEPPER LOAF

*6 servings*

8 ounce loaf Italian or French bread

1/4 cup butter

12 ounces (3 3/4 cups) fresh mushrooms, sliced thin

4 ounces (1 1/2 cups) fresh Portobella mushrooms, sliced (may substitute Shitake)

1 teaspoon garlic, minced

1/4 teaspoon salt

1/4 teaspoon ground black pepper

4 ounces sliced ham

7 ounce jar roasted red peppers, drained and patted dry

4 ounces Provolone cheese, sliced thin

Preheat oven to 350° F. Split loaf lengthwise. Hollow out each half leaving about 1/2 inch bread in the bread crusts. Melt the butter in a large skillet. Add mushrooms, garlic, salt and pepper. Sauté 6 to 8 minutes stirring frequently until mushrooms are tender and the liquid evaporates. Set aside.

Arrange ham in the bottom of each breadcrust half. Top with the mushroom mixture. Add red peppers and cheese. Lay breadcrust halves side by side and fold together slowly. Place on baking sheet. Cover loosely with foil tent and bake 7 to 15 minutes until cheese melts. Slice into 2-inch servings.

### EASY ROASTED RED PEPPERS

*Preheat broiler. Raise the oven rack to top position. Prepare baking sheet with non-stick spray. Halve peppers lengthwise. Remove seeds and membranes. Arrange on baking sheet, skin side up. Place sheet under broiler. Broil peppers 5 to 7 minutes or until skins are charred. Remove peppers and place in a covered bowl or resealable plastic bag. Let cool at least 10 minutes. Peel peppers. Rinse in cool water, if desired. Use peppers as desired.*

### COUNTRY COBBLER

## BRUSCHETTA

*8 to 12 servings*

1 loaf Italian or French bread, sliced into
   1/2 to 3/4-inch thick slices

2 cloves garlic

5 to 6 ripe tomatoes

Fresh basil

2 tablespoons extra virgin olive oil

Preheat oven to 400° F. Toast bread slices on cookie sheet. Remove from oven, rub the toasted side with garlic. Cut and mince the fresh tomatoes by hand into small chunks. Mince the basil and add to tomatoes. Stir in olive oil. Use a slotted spoon and place a spoonful of tomato basil mixture on each garlic toast.

40

***Idea!***

*The key is fresh tomatoes and great olive oil!*

## HOUSTON'S SPINACH DIP
*12 to 16 servings*

1 medium onion, chopped fine

1/4 cup butter or margarine

1 8-ounce package cream cheese

8 ounce Monterey Jack cheese, shredded

2 10-ounce boxes frozen spinach, thawed
   and drained

1 cup artichoke hearts

1/4 cup Parmesan cheese

Preheat oven to 350° F. Sauté onion with butter. To the onion mixture, add cream cheese and Monterey Jack cheese until melted. Stir in spinach and artichoke hearts. Transfer mixture into a 8 x 12-inch greased baking dish. Top with Parmesan cheese. Bake 15 to 25 minutes until cheese is melted. Serve with chips, sour cream and salsa on the side, optional.

41

 *Idea!*

*To insure the right amount of ice for a party, a good standard to use is one pound per person.*

## BLOODY MARY

*Makes 3 quarts*

1 quart Vodka
1/2 cup Worcestershire sauce
1/2 teaspoon horseradish
1/2 teaspoon sugar
1 teaspoon pepper
hot pepper sauce to taste
2 quarts vegetable juice
1 empty gallon jug
fresh lime juice to taste

Combine all ingredients in the gallon jug. Place top back on jug and shake well. Refrigerator for 3 days, shaking the jug daily. Serve with celery stalks and a squeeze of fresh lime.

## SUNSHINE PUNCH

*25 servings*

1 12-ounce frozen orange juice concentrate
1 6-ounce frozen limeade concentrate
1 46-ounce unsweetened pineapple juice
1 cup sugar
1 quart water
2 liters lemon-lime soda

Combine orange juice, limeade, pineapple juice, sugar and water, and place in plastic container with cover. Freeze. Two hours before serving place in punch bowl to thaw. Add lemon-lime soda before serving.

## Spiced Iced Tea

*Makes 1 gallon*

1 quart water
1 cup sugar
12 regular size tea bags or 4 family size tea bags
8 mint leaves, crushed
1 6-ounce can frozen orange juice
1 6-ounce can frozen lemonade

Bring water to a boil, stir in 1 cup of sugar until dissolved, add tea bags and crushed mint leaves. Turn tea off and let brew for 20 minutes. After brewing remove tea bags and mint; stir in orange juice and lemonade; mix well. Pour mixture into gallon container. Add water to make 1 gallon. Chill.

## Coffee Liqueur

*Makes 5 1/2 cups - takes 2 weeks*

2 cups water
1 1/2 cups sugar
1 1/2 cups brown sugar
1/3 cup instant coffee crystals
1 fifth vodka
2 teaspoons vanilla

In sauce pan combine water, sugar and brown sugar. Simmer gently uncovered for 10 minutes. Remove from heat. Stir in coffee and cool. Pour into 2 quart screw top jar. Stir in vodka and vanilla. Cover with lid, let stand at room temperature for 2 weeks.

### Festive Touches for Beverages

·*Fruit kabobs of berries and melon balls*

·*Lemon, lime, pineapple or kiwi wedges for the rims of glasses*

·*Frozen berries*

·*Lemon or lime zest*

·*Mint sprigs*

43

### ICED DESSERT COFFEE
*4 to 6 servings*

1 cup sugar
4 cups espresso or very strong coffee
half and half or light cream, to taste

Add sugar to espresso or coffee while it is hot. Stir to dissolve the sugar and let cool to room temperature. Pour the mixture into a 9 x 13-inch or 8 x 12-inch glass or metal baking pan and place in freezer. Freeze half hour, then stir. Return pan to freezer and stir it every half hour until mixture is frozen. This will take 2 to 3 hours. The mixture will have crystals in it. To serve, scoop the frozen mixture into a clear glass and pour half and half or light cream over the top.

### COFFEE PUNCH
*60 servings*

1 gallon strong coffee
5 teaspoons vanilla extract
5 tablespoons sugar
1 quart cream
2 quarts vanilla ice cream, softened

Combine coffee, vanilla and sugar. Mix until sugar dissolves. Chill. Just before serving, stir in cream and scoops of ice cream.

## BANANA PUNCH

*4 quarts frozen mixture*

6 cups water
2 cups sugar
1/2 cup lemon juice
1 cup orange juice
1 46-ounce can pineapple juice
5 bananas, mashed
2 liters lemon-lime soda

Combine water, sugar, lemon juice, orange juice, pineapple juice and bananas. Freeze. Defrost in refrigerator to slush stage approximately 2 to 3 hours before serving. Add soda when ready to serve.

## EGG NOG

*Makes 4 quarts*

1 quart whipping cream
1 dozen eggs, separated
2/3 cups sugar
1/2 pint whiskey
1/2 pint spiced rum

Separate eggs. Beat egg whites stiff, slowly add sugar to the egg whites; set aside. Beat egg yolks, very slowly, add whiskey and beat until the whiskey has "cooked" the eggs; set aside. Whip cream stiff, add sugar slowly. Fold in all ingredients very slowly. Should be thick consistency.

## SOUTHERN CITRUS SENSATION

*Makes 4 cups*

*1 cup freshly squeezed orange juice*

*1 1/2 cups freshly squeezed grapefruit juice*

*1/2 cup freshly squeezed lemon juice*

*1 cup sugar*

*2 cups ice, crushed or cracked*

*Combine orange juice, grapefruit juice, lemon juice, sugar and ice in a pitcher. Stir and serve.*

45

NOTES:

..............................................

..............................................

..............................................

..............................................

..............................................

..............................................

..............................................

..............................................

..............................................

..............................................

..............................................

..............................................

..............................................

..............................................

..............................................

Bread & Breakfast

## *Holy Trinity Episcopal Church*

Truly one of Gainesville's treasures, the beauty of Holy Trinity Episcopal Church has endeared it to the hearts of local residents. This gothic style church was originally built in 1907. The magnificent stained glass windows were the highlight of this downtown church. The large ascension window in the back of the church provided a brillance everyone enjoyed.

Tragically, on January 21, 1991, this treasure was destroyed by fire. This was a loss felt by the entire community. After several months, clean-up and rebuilding efforts began. The rebuilding effort brought the Gainesville community together and symbolized a renewal of hope for the downtown.

The new church, along with a new parish hall and education building, was completed in 1995, and every effort was made to rebuild it to its original beauty. Luckily, the lovely ascension window from the original church was saved from the fire because it was being repaired at the time. This lovely window once again provides its brillance for those who enter the church.

Holy Trinity Episcopal Church is a Gainesville landmark which has come to symbolize hope and community feeling. Its glorious re-opening following the tragic fire instills hope and a triumphant spirit to all!

THE PRECEDING PAGE PRESENTED BY KITCHEN & SPICE AND OTHER THINGS NICE

# BREAD & BREAKFAST

## PUMPKIN CHOCOLATE CHIP MUFFINS

*Makes 72 mini muffins or
16 to 20 regular muffins*

2 cups flour

2 teaspoons baking powder

2 teaspoons baking soda

1/2 teaspoon salt

1/2 teaspoon cinnamon

4 eggs

2 cups sugar

1 cup oil

2 cups canned pumpkin

1 cup pecans, chopped

1 cup mini chocolate chips

Preheat oven to 350° F. Prepare muffin pan(s) with butter, cooking spray or paper liners. Sift together flour, baking soda, salt and cinnamon. Set aside. Combine eggs, sugar, oil and pumpkin; mix well. Stir in flour mixture until just moistened—do not over mix. Fold in pecans and chocolate chips. Spoon into pan(s), filling each cup two-thirds full. Bake 18 to 24 minutes.

50

## KITTY'S BISCUITS

*Makes 2 1/2 dozen*

2 cups self-rising flour

1 teaspoon sugar

1/2 cup plus 1 rounded tablespoon shortening

3/4 cup very cold milk (buttermilk may be substituted, adding 1/8 teaspoon baking soda)

flour for rolling out and cutting

Preheat oven to 450° F. Sift flour and sugar into bowl and work shortening into flour using hands. Pour milk into mixture, enough to make a soft dough. Handle lightly, using upward motions instead of pressing down. Toss onto floured board and lightly roll out with floured rolling pin to about 1/2 inch in thickness, for fluffy biscuits, 1/4 inch for crusty biscuits. Cut out with small biscuit cutter. Dip cutter in flour frequently for easy cutting. Place biscuits on greased cookie sheet and bake on top rack 5 to 7 minutes or until golden brown. To freeze, place pan of unbaked biscuits in freezer until firm, then package in plastic bags. They will keep as long as two weeks. Take out as many as needed and place on greased cookie sheet and thaw. Follow baking instructions.

51

## FRUITY MUFFINS

*Makes 12 muffins*

1 cup flour

1/2 cup quick oats

1 teaspoon baking powder

1 teaspoon cinnamon

1/4 teaspoon salt

1 large egg

3/4 cup brown sugar

1/4 cup butter or margarine, melted

1 teaspoon vanilla

1 cup apples, diced

1 cup cranberries

1/2 cup raisins

Preheat oven to 350° F. Grease muffin cups or use paper liners. Combine flour, quick oats, baking powder, cinnamon and salt. Mix together and set aside. Combine egg and sugar, whisk until smooth. Whisk in butter and vanilla. Stir in fruit. Fold in flour mixture until just moistened. Spoon batter into prepared muffin pan. Bake 20 to 25 minutes or until brown and firm to the touch.

Do not freeze.

*Note:*
*Other fruit may be substituted to add different flavors (e.g. pears, raspberries, blueberries.)*

## CARAWAY CHEESE MUFFINS

*Makes 12 muffins*

2 cups flour

1 tablespoon baking powder

2 teaspoons sugar

1 1/4 teaspoons salt

1/4 teaspoon dry mustard

1 cup sharp Cheddar cheese, grated

1 large egg

1 cup milk

1/4 cup unsalted butter, melted
    and cooled

1 1/2 teaspoons caraway seeds

Preheat oven to 350° F. In a bowl, sift flour, baking powder, sugar, salt and mustard. Stir in the Cheddar cheese. In a separate bowl, whisk egg, milk and butter. Add mixture to the dry ingredients. Stir batter until just moistened. Do not over mix. Put into 12 well-buttered 1/2 cup muffin pans. Sprinkle with caraway seeds. Bake 25 to 30 minutes or until golden. Cool two minutes in pan. Transfer from pan to rack to cool.

## HERBED GARLIC BREAD

*4 servings*

1/2 cup loosely packed flat leaf Italian
   parsley leaves, chopped course

1/2 teaspoon dried thyme

1 teaspoon fresh lemon juice

2 medium garlic cloves, minced

1/2 teaspoon salt

1/4 teaspoon freshly ground pepper

1/4 cup olive oil

1 12-inch loaf Italian style white bread

Preheat oven to 350° F. Whisk together parsley, thyme, lemon juice, garlic, salt, pepper and olive oil in a small bowl. Using a bread knife, slice loaf into 12 1/2-inch slices without cutting completely through the bottom of the loaf. Brush herb mixture liberally between each slice. Wrap loaf loosely in foil. Heat until warm, about 10 minutes. Serve immediately.

## Tomato Basil Biscuits

*Makes 12 biscuits*

1 cup flour

1/2 teaspoon sugar

1/4 teaspoon salt

2 teaspoons baking powder

4 tablespoons butter, cold and
    cut into 1/2-inch cubes

1/4 cup half-and-half or milk

2 ripe tomatoes, peeled, seeded and chopped
    coarse (1/2 cup)

1/3 cup fresh basil, chopped

Preheat oven to 425° F. Combine flour, sugar, salt and baking powder. Mix well. Cut in butter. Add milk, tomatoes and basil. On a floured surface, roll out dough to 1/2-inch thickness. Cut biscuits with a 2-inch round cutter. Place biscuits one inch apart on greased cookie sheet. Bake 15 minutes.

## CHILE CHEESE GRITS

*10 to 12 servings*

1 1/2 cups grits, cooked according to package directions

2 teaspoons salt

3 eggs, beaten

1 pound Cheddar cheese, shredded

3 teaspoons savory salt

dash hot pepper sauce

dash Worcestershire sauce

dash of paprika

2 4-ounce cans chopped green chilies

Preheat oven to 250° F. Combine all ingredients in medium mixing bowl; mix well. Bake in 9 x 13-inch baking dish for 1 1/2 to 2 hours, or until firm.

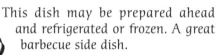

This dish may be prepared ahead and refrigerated or frozen. A great barbecue side dish.

## GRITS CASSEROLE

*6 to 8 servings*

3 1/2 cups milk

1 cup hominy grits

salt and pepper to taste

1/2 cup butter

1 6-ounce roll garlic cheese, cut into
    1/2-inch chunks

2 eggs, beaten

1/2 cup milk

1/2 cup Cheddar cheese, grated

Preheat oven to 375° F. Bring 3 1/2 cups milk to boil in medium saucepan. Gradually stir in grits. Season with salt and pepper. Cook over medium heat, stirring constantly, until thick, about 10 minutes. Remove from heat. Add butter and garlic cheese. Stir until melted. Stir in eggs and 1/2 cup milk. Pour into 2-quart greased casserole. Bake uncovered 30 minutes. Sprinkle cheese over top. Bake 15 minutes longer.

**A BRIDAL BRUNCH**

*Bring on brunch! Its versatility allows it to fit a wide variety of menus. Whether the occasion demands a fancy menu or a casual one, an attractive brunch can be easily prepared with little fuss.*

*Begin with delicious Ham Strata. Its savory flavor goes well with curried fruit and other menu items.*

*Two guaranteed delights to complete the meal are our Coffee Cake and Strawberry Bread.*

*We were also sure to include a Southern classic with a twist.*

*Spiced Tea*
*page 43*

*Curried Fruit*
*page 63*

*Sausage Muffins*
*page 64*

*Grits Casserole*
*page 57*

*Ham Strata*
*page 71*

*Coffee Cake*
*page 67*

*Strawberry Bread*
*page 65*

FLORIDA FOOD
SERVICE

57

## BAKED BLUEBERRY FRENCH TOAST

*4 to 8 servings*

1 loaf Italian or French bread (large, soft loaf not hard, baguette style)

6 eggs

1 1/2 cups milk

1 cup half and half

1 1/2 teaspoons vanilla

1 1/2 teaspoons nutmeg

1/2 teaspoon cinnamon

1 16-ounce can blueberries in heavy syrup or pie filling (may substitute other fruit)

powdered sugar, optional

Night before: Cut loaf in half lengthwise. Slice vertically in half and each half in half again. (Should have eight pieces) Place in buttered 9 x 13-inch baking dish crust side down. Use a blender or hand mixer to combine eggs, milk, half and half, vanilla, nutmeg and cinnamon. Beat until frothy. Pour mixture over bread slices. Cover with plastic wrap and refrigerate overnight.

Next morning: Preheat oven to 350° F. Remove plastic and bake toast for 40 minutes. Meanwhile, heat blueberries in saucepan over medium to low heat. Serve 1 to 2 pieces of toast with warmed blueberries ladled on top. Garnish with sifted powdered sugar.

*Note:*
*This is a great holiday morning breakfast dish since most of the work is done the night before.*

## Egg Casserole

*8 to 10 servings*

8 eggs

1 pound pork sausage, crumbled

1 6-ounce box seasoned croutons

1 1/2 cups Cheddar cheese, grated

1 cup Swiss cheese, grated

1 cup Monterey Jack cheese, grated

1 pint half and half

1 1/2 cups milk

1 1/2 teaspoons dry mustard

salt and pepper to taste

Preheat oven to 325° F. Spray a 9 x 13-inch glass baking dish with non-stick spray. Beat eggs. Fry sausage, drain on paper towels. Combine all ingredients. Mix well. Pour mixture into prepared baking dish. Bake 45 minutes to 1 hour; until a knife inserted into the center comes out clean.

## SOUR CREAM WAFFLES

*6 servings*

3 eggs

2 cups flour

1 1/2 teaspoons brown sugar

1 1/2 teaspoons baking soda

1 teaspoon salt

3 tablespoons butter, melted

1 cup sour cream

1 cup milk

vegetable oil (to grease waffle iron if it is
    not non-stick)

Separate eggs. Beat egg whites until foamy and set aside. Combine flour, brown sugar, baking soda and salt. Mix well. Add egg yolks, butter and sour cream. Mix together and stir in half of milk. Add egg whites and remaining milk. Mix well. Heat waffle iron, brush with oil if necessary. Pour in enough batter to just fill. Close and bake until steaming stops and waffle is golden brown and crisp (2 1/2 to 3 1/2 minutes).

# WAFFLES SUPREME

*4 servings*

1 1/3 cups flour, sifted

2 teaspoons baking powder

1/2 teaspoon salt

2 eggs, separated

1/4 cup sugar

1/2 cup butter, melted (must be real butter)

1 cup milk

Sift together flour, baking powder and salt; set aside. Beat egg yolks until light and foamy. Add sugar and cooled butter. Mix well. Add milk alternately with sifted dry ingredients to egg mixture. Fold in stiffly beaten egg whites. Bake in hot waffle iron.

## EASY SUNSHINE JAM

*Makes 3 cups*

*4 cups fresh blueberries*

*2 cups sugar*

*1 3-ounce package lemon flavor gelatin*

*Combine all ingredients in a large saucepan. Bring to a boil over medium-high heat. Reduce heat to medium and stir for three minutes. Pour mixture into lidded jars. Refrigerate.*

61

## SWEETWATER CREPES

*Recipe from Sweetwater Branch Inn*

5 to 6 servings

1 cup flour

1 tablespoon sugar

pinch of salt

1 cup milk

3 eggs

1/3 cup water

1 tablespoon butter

62

Combine flour, sugar and salt; add milk and blend well. Add eggs, one at a time mixing well with a whisk. Add water and beat well. Heat a non-stick skillet over medium-high heat. Melt butter. Pour enough batter to cover bottom of pan with a thin coating. Immediately start to spread the batter as thinly and evenly as possible by moving pan around. Spread the batter onto the sides of the skillet to facilitate turning the crepe. Let the crepe cook until it browns; about one minute. Turn crepe with a plastic spatula. Cook one minute. Stack cooked crepes.

Spread a thin layer of cream cheese on half of crepe and a thin layer of blackberry preserves on the other half. Place the crepe on a warmed flat skillet to warm the crepe before serving. You may fold it into fourths or roll it up. Sift powdered sugar over top.

## CURRIED FRUIT

*6 to 8 servings*

1/3 cup butter, softened

3/4 cup brown sugar

4 teaspoons curry powder

1 16-ounce can pear halves

1 15-ounce can apricot halves, peeled

1 20-ounce can pineapple chunks

1 16-ounce can peach halves

other fruits such as kumquats or cherries
    may be added

Preheat oven to 325° F. Mix butter, brown sugar and curry powder. Drain the canned fruits and place in 9 x 13-inch baking dish. Spread sugar mixture over fruits. Bake for 1 hour. Can be baked once and reheated and it's even better!

## BLUE CHEESE BISCUITS

*Makes 1 dozen*

1 cup blue cheese, softened

1/2 cup butter, softened

1 cup flour

1/2 cup pecans or walnuts, chopped coarse

1/2 cup pecans or walnuts, chopped fine

Preheat oven to 350° F. Cream blue cheese and butter together. Add flour and coarsely chopped nuts. Roll teaspoons of mixture into balls and roll in finely chopped nuts. Flatten slightly on baking sheet. Bake 15 to 17 minutes.

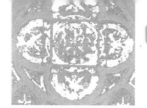
## SAUSAGE MUFFINS

*Makes 1 dozen*

1/2 pound sausage

2 cups flour

2 tablespoons sugar

1 tablespoon baking powder

1/4 teaspoon salt

1 1/4 cups milk

2 eggs, beaten

1/4 cup butter

1/2 cup Cheddar cheese, shredded

non-stick cooking spray

Preheat oven to 375° F. In a large skillet, brown sausage and set aside. Combine flour, sugar, baking powder and salt; set aside. Combine milk, eggs and butter. Add to dry mixture, stirring until moistened. Stir in sausage and cheese. Place paper baking cups in muffin pans or coat with non-stick cooking spray. Spoon batter into cups and bake 15 to 20 minutes.

## STRAWBERRY BREAD

*Makes 2 loaves*

3 cups flour

1 teaspoon baking soda

1 teaspoon salt

2 teaspoons cinnamon

2 cups sugar

3 eggs, well beaten

2 10-ounce packages frozen strawberries, thawed

1 1/4 cups vegetables oil

1 cup walnuts, chopped; optional

Preheat oven to 350° F. Sift together flour, baking soda and salt. Stir in cinnamon, sugar, eggs, strawberries, oil and nuts. Mix gently until just combined. Pour into greased loaf pans. Bake 1 hour or until toothpick inserted comes out clean.

### SPICED APPLE MUFFINS

*Makes 12 large muffins*

*2 1/2 cups sifted flour*

*1 teaspoon salt*

*1/2 teaspoon nutmeg*

*1 egg*

*1/3 cup shortening, melted*

*1 cup apples, chopped*

*3 1/4 teaspoons baking powder*

*1/2 teaspoon cinnamon*

*1/4 cup sugar*

*1 1/4 cup milk*

*1 cup apple wedges*

*Sift flour with baking powder, salt, spices and sugar. Combine beaten egg, milk and shortening. Turn liquids into dry ingredients and stir vigorously until all flour is dampened. The batter will look lumpy. Fold chopped apples carefully into mixture. Pour into greased muffin tins. Lay an apple wedge on top of each muffin. Sprinkle with mixture of:*

*1/4 teaspoon nutmeg,*

*1/4 cup cinnamon*

*2 tablespoons sugar.*

*Bake in hot oven at 400° F for 25 to 30 minutes.*

*This recipe is from the Junior League of Gainesville's first cookbook* Culinary Crinkles.

SWEETWATER BRANCH INN

## BANANA NUT BREAD

*Makes 1 loaf*

1/4 pound butter or margarine, softened

1 cup sugar

4 large bananas, very ripe

2 eggs, beaten

2 cups flour

1 teaspoon baking powder

1/2 teaspoon baking soda

1/4 teaspoon salt

3/4 teaspoon vanilla

1/2 cup chopped nuts

Preheat oven to 350° F. Cream butter and sugar together. Mash bananas. Add bananas, eggs and all other ingredients to butter and sugar. Pour into greased 9-inch loaf pan. Bake slowly 40 to 45 minutes until golden brown.

66

## COFFEE CAKE

*10 to 12 servings*

1 cup butter

2 cups sugar

2 egg yolks, slightly beaten

2 cups flour, sifted

1/2 teaspoon salt

1 teaspoon baking powder

8 ounces sour cream

2 egg whites, beaten into stiff peaks

1 teaspoon vanilla

1/2 cup brown sugar

1/2 cup pecans, chopped

1 tablespoon cinnamon

Preheat oven to 350° F. Cream butter and sugar; stir in egg yolks; mix well and set aside. Combine flour, salt and baking powder. Alternately add flour mixture and sour cream to butter mixture. Fold in stiffly beaten egg whites and vanilla. Pour half of batter into a greased tube pan. Combine brown sugar, pecans and cinnamon; swirl into batter. Add remaining batter and bake for 60 to 65 minutes.

## CHEESE PUFFS
## WITH GREEN CHILIES

*Makes 30 puffs*

1/2 cup milk

1/2 cup water

8 tablespoons butter, lightly salted

1 cup flour

4 eggs

11/4 cup Swiss cheese, grated

1/2 teaspoon salt

2 tablespoons green chilies, mashed

68

Preheat oven to 400° F. Position oven racks near the top for browning.

Place water, milk, salt and butter in a sauce pan, bring to a full boil. Remove pan from heat; add flour and stir. Return to medium heat, stirring constantly, until the dough draws together into one mass. At this point it will also begin to coat the bottom of the pan with a film as you are stirring.

Remove saucepan from heat, allowing to cool a minute or two. Stir in one egg at a time, thoroughly incorporating each egg, until all eggs have been added. Stir in the cheese and mashed chilies.

Drop the still-warm dough by tablespoons 1/2 inch apart onto 3 ungreased baking sheets. Sprinkle a pinch of Swiss cheese on top of each puff and place in oven. Immediately turn oven down to 375° F and bake 15 to 20 minutes, or until golden brown. Reduce heat to 350° F and let the puffs dry out for another 5 minutes, but do not over brown them.

## SAUSAGE PINWHEELS

*Makes 20 pinwheels*

1 can crescent rolls (8 count)

1 16-ounce breakfast sausage

Divide crescent roll rectangle in half at seam. Place on wax paper pinching the seams closed. Put sausage on each rectangle and roll up and roll in wax paper. Refrigerate for at least 2 hours. Cut into 1/4-inch thick slices. Place on ungreased cookie sheet and bake 20 minutes or until lightly browned.

Rolls may be frozen and sliced with an electric knife.

## CHEDDAR BREAD

*8 servings*

1 loaf French or Italian bread

1 teaspoon red pepper sauce

1/2 cup butter, softened

1 teaspoon thyme

1/2 medium red onion, sliced thin

2 cups Cheddar cheese, shredded

Preheat oven to 400° F. Slice bread in half lengthwise. Combine red pepper sauce, butter and thyme. Spread mixture on both halves of bread. Layer onion and cheese on one half; top with the other. Wrap in foil and bake 20 minutes. Slice and serve warm.

## Ham Strata

*12 servings*

20 slices white bread

5 to 6 cups ham, cubed

10 ounces Swiss cheese, shredded

10 ounces sharp Cheddar cheese, shredded

6 eggs

3 cups milk

1/2 teaspoon onion salt

1/2 teaspoon salt

1/2 teaspoon dry mustard

1/2 cup butter, melted

3 cups cornflake crumbs

Preheat oven to 325° F. Trim crusts from bread, then cut 10 slices of bread in half and lay in bottom of greased 9 x 13-inch pan. On top of bread, layer half of the ham. Combine cheeses and layer half of the cheese mixture on top of ham. Repeat layering process with rest of bread, ham and cheese. Combine eggs, milk, onion salt, salt and mustard; pour over mixture in pan. Cover with foil and refrigerate overnight. Before baking, toss cornflake crumbs in melted butter and sprinkle on top of casserole. Bake uncovered 55 minutes. Let stand 10 minutes before cutting into squares.

NOTES:

...............................................................

...............................................................

...............................................................

...............................................................

...............................................................

...............................................................

...............................................................

...............................................................

...............................................................

...............................................................

...............................................................

...............................................................

...............................................................

...............................................................

...............................................................

Soup & Salad

## Matheson Historical Center

Located downtown on the banks of Sweetwater Branch Creek is the Matheson Historical Center, a classic red brick building known since the 1930s as the American League Hall. The Center is a privately funded non-profit archives and museum of Gainesville and Alachua County history, named for the Matheson family, an early Gainesville family. Adjacent to the Center are the Matheson Historical House Museum and Sweetwater Branch Park, a public botanical garden featuring native plants.

Visiting the Matheson Center is like turning the pages of a giant scrapbook of intriguing artifacts such as rare maps, old photographs and postcards, original art and vintage stereo view cards. Dioramas and graphic representations tell the history of Alachua County from the prehistoric era to the present. In the Helen C. Ellerbe Library and Mark V. Barrow Archives, the curious can thumb through volumes of state and area history. The Center provides Gainesville with an important link to its rich heritage.

# SOUP & SALAD

### CREAMY BUTTERNUT BISQUE

*4 to 6 servings*

2 medium leeks, carefully washed and chopped (white parts only)

1 cup celery, chopped

1 cup carrots, chopped

4 tablespoons butter

1 medium butternut squash, peeled, seeded and cut into chunks

1 2-inch piece of fresh ginger root, peeled and minced

4 cups chicken stock (or water)

1/2 cup light cream or half-and-half

salt and pepper to taste

freshly grated nutmeg and toasted pecans for garnish (optional)

Sauté leeks, celery and carrots in butter for 10 minutes. Add squash, ginger root and stock or water. Simmer 20 to 30 minutes, or until vegetables are tender. Let cool slightly. Purée in blender or food processor until smooth. Return to pot and stir in cream. Heat through, but do not allow to boil. Season with salt and pepper. When serving, top with freshly grated nutmeg and toasted pecans if desired.

 **Idea!**
An electric hand blender can quickly purée soups and sauces directly on the stove saving time and clean-up!

## TURKEY AND
## WILD RICE CHILI
*6 to 8 servings*

1 tablespoon canola oil

1 medium onion, chopped

1 clove garlic, minced

1 1/4 pounds boneless, skinless turkey or
   chicken, cut into 1/2 inch pieces

2 cups cooked wild rice

1 15-ounce can great Northern beans,
   drained

1 11-ounce can white corn

2 4-ounce cans diced green chilies

1 14 1/2-ounce can low sodium
   chicken broth

1 teaspoon ground cumin

2 teaspoons chili powder

1 teaspoon salt

hot pepper sauce

Monterey Jack cheese, shredded

sour cream

parsley

Heat oil in a large skillet over medium heat;
add onion and garlic. Sauté until tender. Add
turkey, wild rice, beans, corn, chilies, broth
and cumin. Cover and simmer over low heat
30 minutes or under turkey is tender. Stir in
hot pepper sauce to taste. Serve with cheese
and sour cream. Garnish with parsley, if desired.

*In 1996, the Junior
League of Gainesville
held it's first annual
"Run for the Children"
5k run. Held in
conjunction with the
Florida Track Club,
serious runners and
not-so-serious runners
as well as avid walkers
enjoyed the 5k course
at Santa Fe Community
College. Participants
were assigned numbers
and officially clocked.
Entertainment and fun
competitions for
children were
also featured.*

*Community and family
involvement have
helped make this
fundraiser very
successful and likely
to be continued in
the future.*

SAM N. HOLLOWAY
& CO., INC.

### CREAM OF LEEK AND WILD MUSHROOM SOUP

*6 to 8 servings*

2 cups water

4 ounces dried mushrooms
(shitake, porcini, or wild varieties)

3/4 cup unsalted butter

2 shallots, chopped fine

1 medium onion, chopped fine

1 pound leeks, white part only,
chopped fine

1 1/2 pounds fresh Portobella
mushrooms, sliced

1 pound white mushrooms, sliced

4 tablespoons flour

1 cup dry white wine

6 cups chicken stock

1 bay leaf

1 cup heavy cream

1/4 teaspoon salt

white pepper to taste

Bring 2 cups water to a boil in 1 quart sauce pan. Add dried mushrooms, cover and steep the mushrooms for 30 to 40 minutes. Remove stems from mushrooms and slice. Reserve liquid. Set aside.

In large kettle, melt butter, add shallots, onion and leeks, and cook over medium heat for 10 minutes or until softened. Add the Portobella, steeped dried and white mushrooms. Cook, stirring for 10 minutes. Add flour, mixing well; cook for 1 minute more. Whisk in the wine, reserved mushroom liquid, stock and bay leaf. Simmer the mixture covered, for 30 minutes. Remove the bay leaf. Cool slightly.

In blender or food processor, purée half of the mushroom mixture. Add the puréed mixture to the remaining mushroom mixture in the pot. Bring to a slow boil. Turn heat to low and simmer partially covered for 40 minutes longer, stirring occasionally. (This will reduce the liquid slightly to give the broth a fuller flavor.) Add cream and heat through. Add salt and pepper. Adjust seasonings if necessary.

### FRESH SALMON BISQUE
*6 to 8 servings*

3 tablespoons butter

1 large white onion, chopped coarse

4 medium carrots, diced

6 medium celery ribs, diced

2 garlic cloves, minced

1 1/4 cups dry white wine

1 rounded tablespoon tomato paste

1/3 cup flour

2 8-ounce bottles clam juice

2 14.5-ounce cans chicken broth or
    homemade chicken stock

3 tablespoons butter

1 clove garlic, minced

1 pound fresh salmon filet, skin
    and bones removed and cut into
    1/2 inch chunks

1/2 teaspoon salt

1 1/2 cups half-and-half

Melt 3 tablespoons butter in 4-quart pot or Dutch oven. Add onion and sauté on low heat until tender, about 5 to 7 minutes. Add carrots, celery and garlic. Cook until tender. Raise heat to high and add wine. Cook over high heat until all of the wine has been absorbed. Reduce heat to medium. Stir in tomato paste. Add flour, blending well, and cook for 1 minute.

Slowly add clam juice and chicken stock, blending well with a wire whisk making sure no flour lumps form. Bring to boil, reduce to simmer, cover and cook for 15 minutes. Remove from heat and cool to room temperature.

While vegetable stock cools, sauté the remaining 3 tablespoons butter, add garlic and fresh salmon. Sauté over medium high heat until cooked and slightly golden. Add salt to cooked salmon.

Reserving cooled stock, strain vegetables and process until smooth in a food processor or blender. Add cooked salmon and puréed vegetables to stock. Bring to boil, reduce heat, partially cover pan and simmer for approximately 45 minutes or until stock has reduced by one-third. Remove cover, add half-and-half. Adjust salt if necessary.

Garnish with sprigs of watercress or dill.

### MUSHROOM SHRIMP BISQUE
*4 servings*

2 tablespoons green onion, chopped

1/4 cup butter

1/4 teaspoon dry mustard

1/4 teaspoon salt

1/4 cup sifted flour

2 cups half and half

1 4 1/2-ounce can shrimp, undrained

1 4-ounce can mushrooms, sliced

1 egg yolk

1 tablespoon dry sherry

Cook onion in butter just until softened. Stir in mustard, salt and flour. Slowly stir in half-and-half. Cook and stir until mixture boils and thickens. Add undrained shrimp and mushrooms. Beat egg yolk and sherry together. Stir a little of the hot soup into egg mixture, then return mixture to pan. Heat slowly until hot.

82

## POTATO LEEK SOUP

*4 servings*

1/2 teaspoon olive oil

1 medium onion, chopped fine

1/2 pound leeks, chopped fine

1 shallot, minced fine

1 ounce lean ham, diced fine

1 1/4 pounds potatoes, peeled and
  quartered

3 1/2 cups chicken broth

2 tablespoons fresh dill, chopped fine

salt and pepper to taste

Heat oil in large pot over medium heat.
Add onion, leeks, shallot and ham. Cover
and cook for 10 minutes, stirring twice. Add
the potatoes, chicken broth and dill; cover
and simmer 30 minutes, until potatoes are
tender. Remove potatoes and place in blender
with 1 cup of hot broth. Pureé, then whisk
back into remaining soup to thicken. Season
with salt and pepper to taste.

*Note:*
*Soup is better if made ahead because it thickens.*

### COLD CREAM OF
### VIDALIA ONION SOUP

*8 servings*

5 slices lean bacon, cut crosswise into
   1/2-inch strips

1/2 cup unsalted butter

3 pounds (about 10) Vidalia onions,
   sliced thin

8 garlic cloves, minced

4 cups chicken broth

2 cups dry white wine

1 tablespoon fresh thyme
   (or 1 teaspoon dried)

1 bay leaf

1 cup heavy cream, well chilled

1 cup créme fraîche (see sidebar at right)

3 tablespoons fresh lemon juice

1/8 teaspoon hot pepper sauce

1/8 teaspoon nutmeg

salt and pepper to taste

1 cup green onion, sliced thin,
   for garnish

additional cooked bacon, crumbled,
   for garnish

In a heavy saucepan, cook bacon over moderate heat until crisp; transfer to paper towel and drain. Set aside. Add butter to pan and sauté Vidalia onions and garlic over low heat. Cover and stir occasionally. Cook 25 to 30 minutes or until mixture is lightly colored and softened. Add garlic, chicken broth, wine, thyme and bay leaf. Cover and simmer 20 minutes. Discard the bay leaf. In a food processor, purée the mixture in batches. Strain the mixture into a bowl, pressing hard on the solids. Chill covered for 3 to 4 hours or until cold. Whisk in the heavy cream, créme fraîche, lemon juice, hot pepper sauce, and nutmeg. Add salt and pepper to taste. Serve in chilled bowls, sprinkled with bacon and green onion.

CRÈME FRAÎCHE

*A thickened cream used for desserts, sauces and soups. It can withstand higher cooking temperatures before curdling than sour cream. Many grocery stores now carry prepared crème fraîche.*

*In need of a substitute?*

*Use 1 cup whipping cream and 1 teaspoon cultured buttermilk. Mix and heat to 85° F. Let stand at room temperature between 60° F and 85° F. Sauce will thicken. Stir gently. Place in a covered container and refrigerate until needed, no more than a week.*

## SWAMP CHILI

*8 servings*

1/2 pound bacon

8 ounces Italian sausage, crumbled

1 1/2 pounds chuck roast, diced

2 medium onions, chopped

1 green pepper, chopped

1 clove garlic, crushed

1 dried red chili pepper, seeded and crumbled

1 to 2 jalapeno peppers, seeded and chopped

1 to 1 1/2 tablespoons chili powder

1/2 teaspoon salt

1/4 teaspoon dried oregano

1 16-ounce can crushed tomatoes

1 12-ounce can tomato paste

1 1/2 cups water

1 16-ounce can pinto or kidney beans, undrained

In large frying pan cook bacon until crisp, drain and crumble, set aside. Brown sausage in same pan, drain, and set aside, reserving 2 tablespoons drippings. Brown beef, onions, pepper and garlic in pan with drippings. In slow-cooker or Dutch oven, put bacon, sausage, beef, onions, pepper and garlic. Add chili pepper, jalapeno peppers, chili powder, salt and oregano. Stir in crushed tomatoes, tomato paste and water. Cook over low heat 2 to 3 hours, stir in beans, and cook one hour more. The longer it simmers, the better it tastes. Refrigerate leftovers; even better the next day.

# White Cheddar and Ale Soup with Sausage Crostini

*Chef Steve Williams, Steve's Café Americain*

*4 servings*

2 1/2 ounces butter

3/4 cup shallots, minced

2 garlic cloves, minced

5 tablespoons flour

2 cups chicken stock

1 cup pale ale

1 1/2 cups white Cheddar cheese, grated

2 green onions, minced

salt and pepper to taste

Melt butter in large sauce pan. Add shallots and garlic, saute until tender, about 6 minutes. Add flour, stir 4 minutes (do not brown). Whisk in stock and ale. Increase heat; bring to boil, whisking constantly. Reduce heat and simmer until slightly thickened, about 8 minutes. Add cheese a little at a time, whisking until melted and smooth. Add green onions. Season with salt and pepper.

## SAUSAGE CROSTINI

*3-ounces kielbasa, diced*

*1 tomato, chopped coarse*

*2 tablespoons olive oil*

*1 tablespoon balsamic vinegar*

*1 tablespoon fresh basil, minced*

*2 tablespoons shallots, minced*

*salt and pepper to taste*

*8 slices French bread, 1/2-inch thick; toasted*

*Combine sausage, tomato, oil, vinegar, basil and shallots in small bowl. Season with salt and pepper. Spoon sausage mixture onto toasts. Serve floating on soup.*

513

### BISTRO ONION SOUP

*4 servings*

4 large white onions, sliced
   (about 1 1/2 to 2 pounds)
1/4 cup butter
2 tablespoons flour
42-ounces of water
4 chicken bouillon cubes
4 beef bouillon cubes
1/4 teaspoon pepper
1/2 teaspoon sage
2 bay leaves
1/2 cup dry white wine
1/2 cup burgundy
salt to taste
8 1/2-inch thick slices French bread, toasted
8 slices Gruyere or Swiss cheese

Sauté onions in butter in a heavy 4-quart saucepan over medium heat, stirring often, until golden brown, about 20 to 30 minutes. Stir in flour; cook 1 minute. Add water, bouillon cubes, pepper, sage, bay leaves and wines. Heat to boiling. Reduce heat and simmer, partially covered, 30 minutes.

Heat broiler. Ladle soup into four 12 or 16-ounce oven proof soup bowls, and place on a baking sheet. Add 2 slices of toasted bread to each, and cover with 2 slices of cheese. Broil, 6 inches from heat, until cheese is bubbly brown and forms a crust. Place bowls on plates, and serve at once.

*Note:*
*Chicken and beef broth may be substituted for bouillon cubes and water. Add salt to taste.*

## SOUTHWEST BORDER CHOWDER

*8 to 10 servings*

1 onion, chopped
1 green bell pepper, chopped
1 rib of celery, chopped
2 tablespoons butter
1 pound sausage, cooked and drained
1 14-ounce can tomatoes
2 16-ounce cans red kidney beans, drained
1/4 teaspoon garlic powder
1 1/2 teaspoons salt
1/4 teaspoon pepper
2 cups tomato juice
2 16-ounce cans whole kernel corn, drained
1/2 teaspoon thyme
1 teaspoon chili powder
2 whole bay leaves

Sauté onions, peppers and celery in butter in a large pot. Add remaining ingredients. Bring to a boil; reduce heat and simmer 40 minutes. Remove bay leaves. Makes about 3 1/2 quarts. Can be made ahead and refrigerated or frozen.

### PEAR SALAD WITH ARUGULA

*4 servings*

1 head Boston lettuce

2 cups arugula, stems removed

1/3 cup walnuts, toasted

2 red pears, cored and sliced thin with skin
left on (may substitute yellow
or green)

1 small red onion, chopped

1/3 cup French dressing (right)

12 3/4-inch cubes Fontina cheese

20 3/4 to 1-inch cubes French bread

Preheat oven to broil. Tear and toss
Boston lettuce and arugula. Add walnuts,
sliced pears and chopped onion. Toss with
French dressing to lightly coat salad
greens. On wooden skewers, alternate bread
and cheese cubes, beginning and ending with
bread. Place skewers under broiler to soften
cheese and lightly toast bread. Remove
skewers and arrange bread and cheese cubes
on individual plates mounded with greens.

## FRENCH DRESSING
*Makes 3/4 cup*

1/2 cup olive oil

2 tablespoons red wine vinegar

2 tablespoons fresh lemon juice

1 teaspoon sugar

1/2 garlic clove, crushed

1/4 teaspoon pepper, freshly ground

3/4 teaspoon dry mustard

1/2 teaspoon salt

1/8 teaspoon paprika

dash Cayenne pepper

Combine all ingredients in a jar. Cover and shake well. Refrigerate overnight to blend flavors.

## SLICED TOMATOES WITH FETA CHEESE AND BASIL
*4 to 6 servings*

4 to 5 fresh tomatoes, sliced

4 ounces Feta cheese, crumbled

3 tablespoons fresh basil, chopped fine

1/4 cup olive oil

Arrange tomato slices on bottom of serving dish or platter. Sprinkle with crumbled Feta cheese and fresh basil. Drizzle with olive oil. Chill and serve.

### CASHEW SHRIMP SALAD

*8 servings*

- 1 10-ounce package frozen baby peas
- 1 3/4 pounds shrimp, steamed with seasonings, peeled, deveined and chopped into bite-sized pieces
- 2 cups celery, chopped
- 1 cup green onions, chopped
- 1 cup light mayonnaise (not fat-free)
- 1 tablespoon fresh lemon juice
- 1 teaspoon curry powder
- 1 teaspoon garlic powder
- 1 teaspoon salt
- 1 cup unsalted cashews
- 1 5-ounce can chow mein noodles

Combine peas, shrimp, celery, onions, mayonnaise, lemon juice, curry, garlic, and salt. Mix well. Cover and chill 30 minutes or longer. Just before serving, add cashews and noodles; toss. Serve on lettuce leaves with fresh fruit as garnish.

## Avocado and Grapefruit Salad with Limeade Dressing

*4 servings*

4 large lettuce leaves
1 ripe avocado, peeled, pitted and sliced
2 grapefruit, peeled and sectioned
1/2 cup pecans, chopped
4 large strawberries

Place a lettuce leaf on each of four individual salad plates. Divide the avocado and grapefruit among the plates and arrange. Sprinkle chopped pecans over each salad; top with a strawberry. Drizzle dressing over salads and serve.

Dressing:

1/4 cup frozen limeade concentrate, thawed
1/4 cup salad oil
1/4 cup honey
1 tablespoon poppy seed

Whisk all ingredients together until well blended.

93

### BROCCOLI SALAD

*4 to 6 servings*

1 bunch of broccoli flowerets
   (approximately 2 cups)

1 cup raisins

1 cup pecans, chopped

1 cup seedless red or green grapes

Combine broccoli, raisins, pecans and grapes. Stir dressing into broccoli mixture. Mix well. Chill, stirring several times before serving.

Dressing:

1 cup mayonnaise

1/3 cup sugar

1/3 cup milk

2 tablespoons vinegar

Mix ingredients and blend well.

94

### BLUE CHEESE VINAIGRETTE

*Makes 1/2 to 3/4 cup*

1/4 cup olive oil

2 tablespoons white wine vinegar

1 tablespoon lemon juice

1/2 cup blue cheese, crumbled

salt and pepper to taste

Combine olive oil, vinegar, lemon juice and blue cheese. Stir well. Season to taste with salt and pepper.

## SPINACH SALAD

*4 servings*

1 pound fresh spinach, torn into
   bite-sized pieces

1 green bell pepper, chopped

1 bunch green onions, chopped

1 pound mushrooms, sliced

1/2 pound bacon, fried until crisp

Combine spinach, green pepper, green
onions, mushrooms and bacon in bowl. Pour
dressing on top and toss well.

Dressing:

1 cup vegetable oil

5 tablespoons red wine vinegar

4 tablespoons sour cream

2 garlic cloves, minced

1 1/2 teaspoons salt

2 tablespoons sugar

1/2 teaspoon dry mustard

Combine ingredients in a jar and shake well.

---

### "DILLIOUS" CAULIFLOWER SALAD

*6 to 8 servings*

*1 large
head cauliflower*

*2 cups ranch dressing*

*1 tablespoon dill weed*

*Cut cauliflower
into flowerettes.
Steam on stove about
10 minutes until tender
but crunchy.
Drain well.
After draining, put in
9 x 13-inch serving
dish. Cover with
dressing and
sprinkle dill weed
liberally over the top.
Refrigerate 4 hours or
overnight. Do not
transfer to
another dish.*

513

# SOUP & SALAD

96

### CHOPPED SALAD

*4 servings*

1/3 cup frozen green peas

1/2 large head romaine lettuce, chopped

1 medium green bell pepper, chopped

1 medium red bell pepper, chopped

1/3 cup red onion or Vidalia onion, chopped

1/3 cup smoked Gouda cheese, diced

Put the frozen peas in a strainer and run under hot tap water until soft but still bright green. Combine peas with the rest of the salad ingredients in plastic container or bag. Add dressing to taste. Seal container or bag and shake salad until well coated. Unused dressing can be stored in the refrigerator for several weeks.

Dressing:

1/3 cup olive oil

1/3 cup water

1/3 cup red wine vinegar

3 tablespoons Parmesan cheese, grated

1/2 teaspoon sugar

1/2 teaspoon dry mustard

1/2 teaspoon celery seed

1/2 teaspoon oregano

1/4 teaspoon salt

dash fresh ground pepper

Combine ingredients in a jar and shake. Let stand in refrigerator overnight for flavors to blend.

# FRESH SPINACH SALAD

*6 to 8 servings*

1 pound fresh spinach, torn into bite-size pieces

1 cup fresh bean sprouts

3 to 4 fresh mushrooms, sliced thin

1 strip bacon, cooked (Tip: Microwaving between paper towels takes about two minutes)

Combine spinach, bean sprouts and mushrooms in bowl. Crumble bacon strip over salad. Drizzle with dressing to taste and serve.

## Dressing:

1 cup olive oil

1/2 cup red wine vinegar

1/2 cup sugar

1/3 cup ketchup

Combine ingredients in jar. Shake well.

GARDEN GLORIES

*Florida's fabulous climate invites many of us to become backyard gardeners. Among the most popular vegetables grown on these small plots are tomatoes, cucumbers, squash and bell peppers. Enjoy making recipes with your own homegrown veggies or gather some of them from your local supermarket.*

ABBY FROMANG MILON
ATTORNEY AT LAW

97

## ORIENTAL COLESLAW

*4 to 6 servings*

2 packages beef flavor ramen noodles, uncooked

1 16-ounce bag of coleslaw mix

1 cup sunflower seeds

1 small bunch of green onions, chopped (use only white and pale green parts)

1/3 cup of sliced almonds, toasted

Crush dry noodles and combine with coleslaw mix, sunflower seeds and onions in a bowl. Toss with dressing. Sprinkle with toasted almonds. Refrigerate overnight to blend flavors.

Dressing:

1 cup olive oil

1/3 cup red wine vinegar

1/2 cup sugar

2 packets beef seasonings from ramen noodles

Combine ingredients in a jar. Shake well.

## CUCUMBER SALAD

*4 to 6 servings*

2 medium to large cucumbers
1 teaspoon salt
1 tablespoon white vinegar
1 tablespoon sugar
1 tablespoon sesame seed oil
1 teaspoon soy sauce

Peel cucumbers and split them in half lengthwise. Remove pulp and seeds. Slice cucumbers crosswise into thin (1/6 inch) slices. Place in a bowl and sprinkle lightly with salt. Mix gently and let stand 15 minutes. Drain. Add vinegar, sugar, sesame seed oil and soy sauce. Toss gently. Chill before serving.

## BLUE CHEESE DRESSING

*Makes 2 1/4 cups*

1 cup mayonnaise
3/4 cup buttermilk
8 ounces blue cheese, crumbled
7 drops hot pepper sauce
1 tablespoon dried Italian seasoning
1 tablespoon dried parsley flakes
1 teaspoon steak sauce
1 garlic clove, pressed

Combine all ingredients. Mix well. Cover and chill.

### SAUERKRAUT SALAD

*6 to 8 servings*

1 cup sugar
1/2 cup corn oil
1 14.4-ounce can sauerkraut
1/2 cup celery, chopped
1/2 cup green pepper, chopped
1/2 cup carrots, grated
1/2 cup onion, chopped (preferably Italian
   red or Bermuda)

Mix sugar with corn oil and stir well. Pour
over other ingredients and toss. Chill.

*100*

### BLACK BEAN SALAD
### WITH FETA CHEESE

*6 to 8 servings*

2 15-ounce cans black beans, drained and
   rinsed
1/3 cup red onion, chopped
8 ounces Feta cheese, crumbled
1/3 cup green pepper, chopped
3 tablespoons olive oil
1/4 cup fresh lemon juice
3 or 4 sprigs fresh mint or parsley
1/8 teaspoon salt
1/8 teaspoon pepper

Combine all ingredients, toss and refrigerate
at least 30 minutes before serving.

## Bibb Salad with Raspberry-Maple Dressing

*6 servings*

Salad:

2 heads Bibb lettuce, torn

1 purple onion, sliced and separated into rings

1 tomato, sliced into thin wedges

4 ounces blue cheese, crumbled

1/4 cup pine nuts, toasted

Combine lettuce, sliced onion and tomatoes. Arrange on individual salad plates. Sprinkle with blue cheese and pine nuts; drizzle with dressing.

Dressing:

1/4 cup raspberry vinegar

2 tablespoons maple syrup

2/3 cup vegetable oil

Combine vinegar and syrup. Gradually add oil, stirring with a wire whisk.

GRACIOUS GREENS

*Salad greens should be fresh, crisp and of good color. Avoid blemished, limp or yellow greens. Combining several types of greens heightens the flavor of salads.*

*Be gentle when washing salad greens to avoid bruising them. Make sure to thoroughly dry them to prolong storage life and ensure an undiluted dressing. As a rule, tear rather than cut greens.*

*Salad greens should be kept well chilled in the crisper drawer of your refrigerator. The humidity is ideal for them in the crisper.*

GAINESVILLE FAMILY PHYSICIANS

## EGGPLANT AND BELL PEPPER SALAD WITH GOAT CHEESE CROUTONS

*4 servings*

1 large eggplant, cut into 3/4-inch slices

2 small yellow bell peppers, quartered

2 small red bell peppers, quartered

2 small green bell peppers, quartered

Olive oil

salt and pepper to taste

3 tablespoons white wine vinegar

1/2 shallot or green onion, minced

1 garlic clove, minced

1 teaspoon dry mustard

1/2 cup walnut oil or olive oil

1/2 cup walnuts, toasted and chopped

8 1/2-inch slices French bread

1/2 pound soft fresh goat cheese

4 cups mixed greens, torn into
   bite size pieces

1/2 cup walnuts, chopped coarse

102

Preheat broiler or grill to high heat. Brush eggplant slices and bell peppers with oil. Season with salt and pepper. Grill or broil eggplant until soft (about 7 minutes), turning occasionally. Cut eggplant into strips. Peel peppers and cut into strips. (The pepper and eggplant can be prepared up to 4 hours ahead of time. Cover with foil and let stand at room temperature.)

Whisk together vinegar, onion, garlic and mustard in small bowl. Gradually whisk in oil. Stir in toasted walnuts.

To make croutons, preheat oven to 350° F. Arrange bread slices on cookie sheet, bake until toasted (about 10 minutes). Spread goat cheese over croutons and keep warm in oven.

Place greens in a large bowl and toss with enough of the vinegar mixture to taste.

To serve, divide greens among plates, top with eggplant and peppers. Sprinkle with coarsely chopped walnuts. Arrange croutons on sides of plates.

## ZUCCHINI DIP

*Makes 2 cups*

*1 cup zucchini, shredded fine*

*1 cup sharp Cheddar cheese, shredded*

*1/2 cup mayonnaise*

*1/4 cup cream cheese, softened*

*1/2 cup walnuts, chopped*

*1 teaspoon lemon juice*

*1/2 teaspoon salt*

*1/8 teaspoon pepper*

*Squeeze excess moisture out of zucchini by placing in cheesecloth or a strainer. Place zucchini in a bowl; add cheese, mayonnaise, cream cheese, walnuts, lemon juice, salt and pepper, and mix well. Cover and refrigerate at least two hours. Serve with raw veggies or crackers.*

SPA KING

### ANGEL HAIR PASTA SALAD

*6 to 8 servings*

1 pound angel hair pasta
1/2 cup mayonnaise
1/2 cup olive oil, light
3 tablespoons Greek seasoning
4 tablespoons lemon juice
1 green pepper, chopped
4-ounce can sliced black olives, drained

Cook pasta until tender and drain. In large bowl combine mayonnaise, olive oil, Greek seasoning, and lemon juice. Add pasta, green pepper and black olives. Toss well. Chill.

104

### BACON AND RED POTATO SALAD

*8 to 12 servings*

6 cups small red potatoes, unpeeled and cubed
3/4 cup low fat mayonnaise
2 tablespoons Dijon mustard
8 slices bacon, cooked crisp and crumbled
1/3 cup green onions, sliced

Boil potatoes 15 minutes. Drain well. Combine mayonnaise and Dijon mustard in a large bowl. Add potatoes, bacon and onions. Mix together gently. Refrigerate at least 2 hours before serving.

## CURRIED CHICKEN SALAD

*6 servings*

4 cups cooked chicken, diced

1 5-ounce can water chestnuts, drained and
   sliced

1 1/2 cups seedless white grapes

1 cup celery, chopped

1 5-ounce can toasted slivered almonds

1 1/2 cups mayonnaise

2 teaspoons curry powder

2 teaspoons soy sauce

4 tablespoons pineapple juice

salt and pepper to taste

1 can sliced pineapple

lettuce

Combine chicken, water chestnuts, grapes, celery, and almonds; set aside. Blend mayonnaise with curry, soy sauce, pineapple juice and salt and pepper to taste. Combine with chicken mixture. Chill. Serve on pineapple slices and lettuce.

### REFRESHING COPPER PENNIES

*8 to 10 servings*

5 cups carrots, sliced and cooked

1 onion, sliced thin

1 green onion, sliced thin

1 10 3/4-ounce can tomato soup

1 teaspoon seasoned salt

1 teaspoon basil

1/4 cup oil

3/4 cup sugar

1/2 cup vinegar

1 teaspoon prepared mustard

1 teaspoon pepper

1 teaspoon Worcestershire sauce

Combine all ingredients and let stand at room temperature for 4 hours. Marinate in refrigerator overnight. Serve cold on a bed of lettuce.

## PASTA SALAD WITH BLUE CHEESE AND GRAPES

*4 to 6 servings*

8 ounces seashell pasta

2 to 3 cups seedless green grapes, halved

1 8-ounce can pitted ripe olives, drained and halved

3/4 cup green onions, chopped

2 to 3 ounces blue cheese, crumbled

salt and pepper to taste

1/4 teaspoon garlic powder

1 cup mayonnaise

3 tablespoons lemon juice

Cook pasta until tender and drain. Combine pasta, grapes, olives, onions, blue cheese, salt, pepper and garlic powder. Mix mayonnaise and lemon juice until smooth. Pour dressing over salad and toss well. Cover and refrigerate for several hours or overnight. If desired, add more mayonnaise before serving.

513

## RED BLISS POTATO SALAD

*8 to 10 servings*

3 pounds Red Bliss potatoes (or any small red potatoes)

1 pound thick-cut bacon

1/4 cup grainy mustard

1/3 cup red wine vinegar

2 teaspoons sugar

salt and pepper to taste

2/3 cup light olive oil or vegetable oil

1 red onion, diced fine

1 cup Italian parsley, chopped

108

Place unpeeled potatoes in a large pot. Cover with cold water and bring to a boil. Reduce and simmer gently until potatoes are tender when pierced; about 35 minutes. Drain. Cover potatoes with cold water and set aside. Fry bacon until very crisp. Drain on paper towel. When cool, crumble into large pieces and set aside. In a small bowl, whisk together mustard, vinegar, sugar, salt and pepper to taste. Whisk in oil and set aside. Cut potatoes into 1/4-inch thick slices and place in a large bowl. Stir in onion and dressing. Let marinate at least 1 hour. Before serving, stir in parsley and bacon, reserving some to sprinkle on top.

## MANGO VINAIGRETTE
*Makes 1 1/2 cups*

1/2 cup sugar, plus 2 tablespoons

3/4 cup white vinegar

1 small mild onion, grated fine

2 large garlic cloves, pressed or minced

3/4 teaspoon salt

1/2 teaspoon celery seed

1 teaspoon dry mustard

1/2 teaspoon ground cumin

2 tablespoons fresh lime or lemon juice

1 large, ripe Mango, peeled, pitted and
chopped coarse

1/2 cup canola, sunflower or vegetable oil

Combine sugar and vinegar in a saucepan, bring to a boil. Remove from heat and cool to room temperature. Add onion, garlic, salt, celery seed, dry mustard, ground cumin and lime or lemon juice. In a food processor, purée the mango, add the vinegar mixture, purée 45 seconds. Slowly pour in the oil, in a thin stream while processing. Pour into jar and keep refrigerated. Shake well before using.

109

### VINEGAR VARIETY

*Vinegars aren't just for pickling anymore! Experiment with the variety of flavored vinegars to create a new favorite dish. Fruit-flavored vinegars really jazz up soups and salads.*

*Vegetable soups and steamed vegetables such as cauliflower and broccoli come alive with herb vinegars. Balsamic vinegar is tasty when combined with olive oil and freshly grated Mozzarella cheese for an Italian bread dipping sauce. Balsamic vinegar also compliments many fruits. Try it on strawberries for a unique twist.*

*Try this vinaigrette recipe over salads or chicken— it's s-o-o good!*

### BALSAMIC VINAIGRETTE
*Makes 1 1/2 cups*

*4 cloves garlic, peeled*

*6 tablespoons balsamic vinegar*

*2 tablespoons rice wine vinegar*

*3 tablespoons sugar*

*2 tablespoons Dijon mustard*

*1 1/2 teaspoons of Worcestershire sauce*

*1 teaspoon freshly ground black pepper*

*1 teaspoon salt*

*1 teaspoon dried oregano*

*1 cup extra-virgin olive oil*

*In a blender, combine all ingredients except olive oil. Blend until mixture is smooth. Add oil in a thin stream while blender is running. Blend until smooth. Pour into a vinaigrette bottle or similar container.*

ROBBINS EYE CLINIC

## PARMESAN CAESAR TOSSED SALAD
*Makes 2 1/2 cups*

1 green pepper, chopped

1 medium onion, chopped

1 2-ounce jar green olives, sliced

3/4 cup Parmesan cheese, grated

1 8-ounce bottle Caesar dressing

Head of Romaine lettuce

Mix green pepper, onion, green olives, Parmesan cheese, Caesar dressing together in a plastic container with lid. Refrigerate overnight. When ready to serve, pour over Romaine lettuce and toss.

## TORTELLINI SALAD
*4 servings*

8 ounces tortellini cheese pasta, cooked

8 ounces spinach leaves, torn

1 bunch green onions, chopped fine

8 ounces Mozzarella cheese, shredded

3 tablespoons herbs de Provence

2 teaspoons pepper

1/2 cup white vinegar

1/2 cup olive oil

2 tablespoons Dijon mustard

Combine pasta, spinach, onions and cheese in large bowl; set aside. Whisk together herbs de Provence, pepper, vinegar, olive oil and Dijon mustard. Pour over pasta and toss. Marinate at least 3 hours. Serve chilled.

## FAVORITE FAT-FREE DRESSING
*Makes 1/2 cup*

1/4 cup low sodium soy sauce

1/4 cup orange juice

1 clove garlic, crushed

Combine soy sauce, orange juice and garlic together in a jar with a lid. Shake well before serving. Serve over red or green leafy lettuce, or Romaine lettuce.

## CILANTRO-LIME VINAIGRETTE
*Makes 3/4 cup*

2 1/2 tablespoons sugar

1/4 cup olive oil

2 tablespoons rice vinegar

2 1/4 tablespoons fresh lime juice

1 clove garlic, pressed

1 shallot, minced

2 1/2 teaspoons fresh cilantro, chopped

Combine sugar, olive oil, rice vinegar, lime juice, garlic, shallot and cilantro in a jar. Cover tightly and shake well. Chill.

## BLACK BEAN AND RICE SALAD

*8 servings*

2 2/3 cups canned chicken broth

1 1/3 cups long-grain rice

1 15 to 16-ounce can black beans, drained and rinsed

1/4 pound plum tomatoes, seeded and chopped

1 red pepper, chopped

1 cup red onion, chopped

1/4 cup balsamic vinegar

3 tablespoons olive oil

2 tablespoons fresh basil, chopped (or 2 teaspoons dried)

1 tablespoon fresh garlic, chopped

salt and pepper to taste

Bring broth to a boil, stir in rice. Reduce heat to low; cover and cook until broth is absorbed and rice is tender; about 20 minutes. Transfer rice to a large bowl and cool for 15 minutes. Add beans, tomatoes, pepper and onion. Whisk vinegar, oil, basil and garlic together. Add to rice and vegetables and toss to blend. Season with salt and pepper. Serve warm or at room temperature.

## SWEET AND SPICY BEANS

*8 to 10 servings*

1 can black beans, rinsed and drained

1 can black eyed peas, rinsed and drained

1 can red kidney beans, rinsed and drained

1 can corn, drained

1 2-ounce jar pimento,
   chopped and drained

3 to 4 green onions, sliced
   (including the green portions)

1/4 cup and 2 tablespoons red wine vinegar

1/4 cup and 2 tablespoons vegetable oil

1/4 cup and 2 tablespoons sugar

3/4 to 1 teaspoon Cayenne pepper

1/4 teaspoon salt

Toss black beans, black eyed peas, red kidney beans, corn, pimento and onion together; set aside. In bowl blend vinegar, oil, sugar, Cayenne pepper and salt. Pour over bean mixture and chill for 2 to 4 hours. This may be made a day ahead.

### SPRINGTIME VEGETABLE SALAD

*12 to 16 servings*

Herb Marinade, recipe follows

1 1/2 cups fresh mushrooms, sliced

1 1/2 pounds fresh asparagus, cut in two inch pieces, and blanched until tender crisp

1 16-ounce can garbanzo beans

1/2 cup small ripe black olives, pitted

1/2 cup pimento stuffed green olives, sliced

1 small onion, thinly sliced

2 heads iceberg lettuce, cored, rinsed, drained and chilled

1 14-ounce can artichoke hearts

cherry tomatoes

parsley

Combine Herb Marinade with the mushrooms, asparagus, garbanzo beans, olives, onion and artichokes. Chill for 1 hour, turning occasionally. Drain, reserving marinade and place marinated vegetables in serving bowl. Prepare Creamy Vegetable dressing. Cut lettuce into wedges and arrange on individual salad plates. Garnish with cherry tomatoes and parsley. Spoon marinated vegetables over wedges; serve Creamy Vegetable Dressing on the side.

Herb Marinade:
Makes about 2 1/4 cups

1 1/2 cups oil
1/2 cup red wine vinegar
3 tablespoons light corn syrup
2 teaspoons seasoned salt
1 tablespoon dried basil
1/2 teaspoon seasoned pepper

Combine all ingredients in a 1 quart jar, cover and shake to blend.

Creamy Vegetable Dressing:
Makes 2 cups
1/2 cup reserved Herb Marinade
1 cup mayonnaise
1/4 cup green pepper, chopped
1/4 cup pimento, chopped
1 tablespoon green onion, chopped
1 tablespoon parsley, chopped

In small bowl, gradually stir reserved marinade into mayonnaise. Add remaining ingredients and mix well.

# SOUP & SALAD

NOTES:

..................................................................

..................................................................

..................................................................

..................................................................

..................................................................

..................................................................

..................................................................

..................................................................

..................................................................

..................................................................

..................................................................

..................................................................

..................................................................

..................................................................

Side Dishes

## Hippodrome State Theatre

An evening tour of Gainesville could lead you to the Hippodrome State Theatre. It is housed in a statuesque three story columnar building, which was once the Gainesville United States Post Office and was placed on the National Registry of Historic Places in 1973.

This non-profit regional theatre, nationally recognized for artistic achievement and community programming, presents creativity at its best. It is a professionally staged theatre where actors from all over the country come to perform, an improvisational theatre for young audiences and a cinema for first-run artistic releases.

From its opening in 1973 to an audience of eight in a converted convenience store, the Hippodrome now opens to more than 200,000 audience members each year. If you are lucky enough to catch a play, you will experience theatre at its best. Come enjoy this Gainesville entertainment gem!

# SIDE DISHES

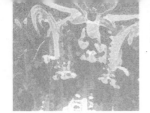

### SHREDDED POTATOES AU GRATIN

*8 to 10 servings*

2 cups sharp Cheddar cheese, shredded

1 cup Mozzarella cheese, shredded

8 medium to large baking potatoes

2 cups whipping cream

1 teaspoon salt

1/4 cup soft bread crumbs

1 tablespoon melted butter or margarine

Preheat oven to 350° F. Combine Cheddar and Mozzarella cheeses and set aside. Place potatoes in large pot, cover with water, bring to a boil and cook 10 minutes. Drain and cool.

Peel and coarsely shred potatoes. Lightly grease a 2 1/2-quart casserole dish. Layer bottom of dish with half of the potatoes, top with half of the cheese mixture and repeat. Combine whipping cream and salt; pour over potatoes and cheese. Sprinkle with bread crumbs and drizzle with melted butter or margarine. Bake uncovered 45 minutes to 1 hour.

## ASPARAGUS AND MUSHROOMS AU GRATIN

*8 servings*

2 15-ounce cans asparagus spears with
    liquid

2 tablespoons butter, divided

1 4-ounce can mushroom pieces with liquid

1 cup light cream

2 eggs

2 tablespoons flour

1/4 teaspoon salt

1/4 teaspoon pepper

1/2 pound Cheddar cheese, grated

paprika to taste, optional

Sauté asparagus and liquid with 1 tablespoon butter until liquid is reduced. Set aside. Sauté mushrooms and liquid with 1 tablespoon butter until liquid is reduced. Set aside. Combine cream, eggs, flour, salt and pepper until foamy. In a buttered 1-quart baking dish, layer 1/3 of the cheese, the asparagus, 1/3 of the cheese, and the mushrooms. Add the cream mixture. Let stand for 30 minutes. Preheat oven to 350° F. Top with remaining cheese. Sprinkle with paprika (optional). Bake 35 minutes (until just set). Serve immediately.

 ***Idea!***

*Use fresh asparagus spears*

121

# SIDE DISHES

### HOMINY CASSEROLE

*8 servings*

2 20-ounce cans hominy, drained

3 tablespoons onion, grated

1 1/2 cups sour cream

1 1/2 cups shredded Monterey Jack cheese

1 4-ounce can chopped green chilies, drained

salt to taste

1/2 cup bread or cracker crumbs, crushed fine

Preheat oven to 350° F. Combine hominy, onion, sour cream, cheese, chilies and salt. Mix together and place in buttered baking dish. Top with bread crumbs. Bake 30 minutes.

### SPINACH SIDE DISH

*4 to 6 servings*

1/4 cup olive oil

2 garlic cloves, crushed

2 large packages fresh spinach, washed and torn into small pieces

1 egg

8 tablespoons Parmesan cheese

4 tablespoons Feta cheese, crumbled (optional)

salt and pepper to taste

Heat olive oil in skillet over medium heat and add crushed garlic. Sauté for 7 to 8 minutes. Stir in spinach and sauté for 3 minutes. Break the egg into the spinach and scramble until the white of the egg is set. Fold in the Parmesan cheese. Top with optional Feta cheese. Serve immediately.

## MUSHROOMS FLORENTINE

*6 servings*

2 10-ounce packages chopped frozen spinach

1/2 teaspoon salt

1/4 cup onion, chopped

6 tablespoons butter or margarine, melted and divided

1 cup white Cheddar cheese, grated and divided

1 pound mushrooms, sliced

1/4 teaspoon garlic powder

Preheat oven to 350° F. Cook spinach according to directions. Drain and squeeze dry. Spoon into shallow casserole. Sprinkle spinach with salt, onion, 2 tablespoons butter and 1/2 cup grated cheese.

Sauté mushrooms in four tablespoons of butter until tender. Spoon mushrooms over cheese layer. Sprinkle with garlic powder and top with 1/2 cup cheese. Bake 20 to 25 minutes.

### GUARDIAN AD LITEM

*The Guardian Ad Litem Program helps improve the lives of abused and neglected children. This representative agency for the courts began as a coalition in 1980 through the efforts of Junior League members. It has expanded to include all Florida judicial circuit courts.*

*Guardian Ad Litem volunteers represent the best interests of an assigned child before the courts, social services and the community. They deal with alleged or confirmed cases of child abuse, conducting an independent investigation to provide valuable information to the court. This enables the judges to make a decision that is best for the child.*

*These community volunteers are vital spokespersons on behalf of abused and neglected children. It is through their efforts this program successfully reaches out to the precious children who so desperately need to be heard.*

JAMES D. SALTER
ESQUIRE

### EASTERN RICE MEDLEY

*12 side servings, or 6 to 8 entrees*

3 tablespoons butter or margarine

1 teaspoon whole cumin seed

1 to 2 sticks of cinnamon

3 to 4 whole cloves

2 large onions, sliced thin

3 1/2 cups water

1/2 cup frozen french-cut green beans

1/2 cup frozen green peas

1/2 cup carrots cut lengthwise,
    1 1/2 inches long

1/2 cup cauliflower, chopped

1/2 cup chopped potatoes

1 teaspoon Cayenne pepper

salt to taste

2 cups uncooked basmati rice (if using
    regular white rice, increase water
    to 4 cups)

1/2 to 3/4 cup raw cashews, chopped

1/4 cup yellow raisins

1 tablespoon butter

In pan, melt butter with cumin, cinnamon and cloves. Sauté onions in butter and spice mixture until lightly browned.

In large pot with lid, boil the water with the green beans, peas, carrots, cauliflower and potatoes. Add Cayenne pepper and salt to taste.

Add rice to onions and heat over low heat 1 to 2 minutes; do not brown rice. Add rice and onion mixture to boiling water with vegetables. Return quickly to a boil. Cover and reduce heat to low and simmer until done, about 15 to 20 minutes.

Sauté the nuts and raisins in 1 tablespoon of butter and use to garnish rice.

## CASHEW-CHUTNEY RICE

*6 to 8 servings*

1 cup celery, diced
3/4 cup onion, diced
6 tablespoons butter
5 cups chicken broth
2 cups long grain white rice, uncooked
1 cup cashews, chopped coarse
1/2 cup mango chutney
3/4 teaspoons pepper

Preheat oven to 350° F. Sauté celery and onion in butter until transparent. Add chicken broth and bring to a boil. Put rice and cashews in a greased 9 x 13-inch baking dish. Add chutney and broth mixture. Add pepper. Stir and cover with foil. Bake 45 minutes to 1 hour.

126

## OKRA AND TOMATOES

*8 to 10 servings*

1/2 pound bacon, diced

1 1/2 tablespoons garlic, minced

2 large onions, chopped

2 pounds fresh okra, sliced

3 pounds fresh tomatoes, chopped

2 tablespoons salt

1 tablespoon black pepper

1 1/2 tablespoons sugar

2 tablespoons fresh basil, minced

Cook bacon over medium heat until it begins to brown. Add minced garlic and chopped onion. Sauté until transparent. Add okra and cook five minutes. Add tomatoes, salt, pepper, sugar and basil. Cook until tender, approximately 25 minutes.

# SIDE DISHES

128

## PARMESAN SCALLOPED POTATOES

*12 servings*

3/4 cup Parmesan cheese, grated

3 tablespoons fresh marjoram, chopped
  or 1 tablespoon dried

1 teaspoon salt

3/4 teaspoon garlic powder

1/4 teaspoon nutmeg, ground

1/4 teaspoon black pepper, ground coarse

5 large baking potatoes, peeled and
  sliced thin

3 cups whipping cream

3/4 cup water

3 tablespoons Parmesan cheese, grated

1 1/2 tablespoons fresh marjoram, chopped
  (or 1 1/2 teaspoon dried)

Preheat oven to 350° F. Combine Parmesan cheese, marjoram, salt, garlic powder, nutmeg and pepper in a small bowl; set aside. Arrange 1/3 of potato slices in a lightly greased shallow 3-quart baking dish and sprinkle with 1/2 of cheese mixture. Repeat layers with remaining potatoes and cheese, ending with potatoes on top. In a separate bowl, combine whipping cream and water; pour over top layer. Sprinkle with 3 tablespoons Parmesan cheese and 1 1/2 tablespoons fresh marjoram. Cover and bake 1 1/2 hours. Uncover and bake another 30 minutes or until potatoes are tender. Let stand 10 minutes before serving.

## STIR-FRIED CARROTS WITH PINEAPPLE

*6 to 8 servings*

1 pound carrots, peeled and sliced thin

2 tablespoons butter

1 tablespoon oil

1 medium onion, chopped fine

1/2 inch piece fresh ginger, peeled and grated fine

1 garlic clove, crushed (optional)

1 7-ounce can pineapple in natural juices, chopped

2 tablespoons pineapple juice

salt and pepper to taste

Blanch the carrots in boiling water for 2 minutes and drain thoroughly. In heavy frying pan, heat butter and oil. Add onion, ginger and garlic. Cook over medium high heat for 2 to 3 minutes until mixture begins to brown. Add carrots, lower heat and sauté for 5 minutes, stirring frequently. Add pineapple pieces, juice and seasonings. Continue to cook for 5 to 6 minutes or until carrots are just tender, but still crisp.

## ONION CASSEROLE
*16 servings*

31 saltine crackers, crumbled

1/2 cup butter, melted

3 cups onions, sliced thin

1/4 cup butter

2 cups Swiss cheese, grated

3 eggs, beaten

1 1/2 cups milk

1/2 teaspoon salt

1/2 teaspoon pepper

Preheat oven to 350° F. Mix cracker crumbs with 1/2 cup melted butter. Press into a 9 x 13-inch glass baking dish. Sauté onions in 1/4 cup of butter until tender. Spoon evenly over cracker mixture and top with cheese. (May be prepared in advance to this point).

Just prior to baking, mix beaten eggs with milk and seasonings. Pour over cheese and onion mixture. Bake for 30 minutes or until custard is set.

## Mozzarella and Tomato Crostini

*6 servings*

2 tablespoon butter or margarine

6 slices white sandwich bread

3 (ripe) plum tomatoes, sliced

1 tablespoon extra virgin olive oil

dried oregano

salt and pepper to taste

10 ounces Mozzarella cheese

12 anchovy fillets in olive oil, drained
  (optional)

Preheat oven to 350° F. Butter the bread slices on one side and cut in half. Lay the bread pieces on a baking sheet, buttered side up. Place the tomato slices in a shallow dish and sprinkle with olive oil, oregano, salt and pepper. Toss gently. Cut the Mozzarella into 12 thin slices to fit bread pieces and top each piece of bread with a slice of Mozzarella. Place anchovy fillet on top of each cheese slice. Place 1 or 2 tomato slices on top. Bake until Mozzarella is melted, about 5 minutes.

131

# SIDE DISHES

### BAKED SWEET POTATOES
*8 servings*

3 cups mashed sweet potatoes, cooked

1/2 cup butter or margarine

1 teaspoon vanilla

1 teaspoon cinnamon

1 cup sugar

1 cup brown sugar

1/3 cup flour

1 cup pecans, chopped

1/2 cup butter or margarine, melted

132

Preheat oven to 350° F. Mix together sweet potatoes, 1/2 cup butter, vanilla, cinnamon and sugar. Place in 9 x 13-inch baking dish. Bake 20 minutes. Mix together brown sugar, flour and pecans. Sprinkle sugar mixture over potatoes and top with 1/2 cup melted butter. Bake 10 minutes.

Even if you don't like sweet potatoes you will like this dish!

## PARISIAN CAULIFLOWER AU GRATIN

*6 to 8 servings*

1 head cauliflower

2 tablespoons butter

2 tablespoons flour

2 cups milk, do not use skim, can use 1% or 2%

1 teaspoon salt

1/2 teaspoon nutmeg

1/2 teaspoon pepper

1 cup Gruyère or Emmenthaler Swiss cheese, grated

1/2 cup Gruyère or Emmenthaler Swiss cheese, grated; for topping

Preheat oven to 425° F. Cut cauliflower into small pieces, steam until tender (15 to 20 minutes); set aside. Melt butter, stir in flour. Pour in milk and blend well, stirring constantly until mixture begins to bubble. Remove from heat. Add salt, nutmeg and pepper, blend well. Add 1 cup cheese a little at a time, mixing well with each addition. Place cauliflower in a 3-quart casserole. Pour cheese sauce evenly over cauliflower. Sprinkle remaining 1/2 cup cheese on top. Bake 15 to 20 minutes until brown and bubbly.

### TERRIFIC TAILGATING MENU

*Enjoy your own tailgating celebration with some of the munchies listed below. We also share some tailgating tips to help make your pre-game festivities a success.*

Down South Barbecue
page 152

Sweet and Spicy Beans
page 113

Oriental Cole Slaw
page 98

Red Bliss Potato Salad
page 108

Bloody Mary's
page 42

Buffalo Wings
page 18

Garbage Dip
page 24

Pumpkin Squares
page 228

Peanut Butter Chocolate Squares
page 231

LENTZ
FINANCIAL GROUP

133

# SIDE DISHES

## SQUASH CASSEROLE
*4 to 6 servings*

2 to 3 cups yellow crook neck or zucchini
  squash, sliced

1 small onion, sliced

1/2 teaspoon garlic powder

1 egg, beaten slightly

1/2 cup margarine

1/2 cup lowfat mayonnaise

1 tablespoon sugar

1/2 cup sharp Cheddar cheese, grated

1/2 cup cracker crumbs

1/4 teaspoon Cayenne pepper

salt and pepper to taste

onion powder to taste

1/2 cup sharp Cheddar cheese, grated

1/2 cup cracker crumbs

3 to 4 strips of bacon, fried crisp

Preheat oven to 350° F. Place squash and
onion in a steaming basket and sprinkle with
garlic powder. Cover and steam approximately
10 minutes until squash is tender, but not
mushy. Combine egg, margarine, mayonnaise
and sugar; mix with squash and onions. Stir
just until mixed. Add 1/2 cup grated cheese
and 1/2 cracker crumbs. Stir until mixed.
Add Cayenne pepper, salt, pepper and onion
powder; mix. Spray a 1 1/2-quart baking dish
with non-stick spray. Pour mixture into
dish. Top with remaining cheese and cracker
crumbs. Bake 20 minutes. Crumble bacon
over top during last few minutes of cooking.

*134*

## CRAZY MIXED UP BEANS

*6 to 8 servings*

1 16-ounce can pork and beans

1 15-ounce can lima beans

1 16-ounce can navy beans

1 15 1/2-ounce can kidney beans

1 15-ounce can pinto beans

1 tablespoon vinegar

1 onion, sliced

1 green pepper, sliced

1 1/2 cups brown sugar

2 tablespoons prepared mustard

1/2 pound sliced bacon

Preheat oven to 350° F. Mix beans, vinegar, onion and green pepper together and put in 2-quart casserole dish. Cover with brown sugar 1/2 to 1-inch thick and dollop with mustard. Cover entire dish with bacon. Bake two hours.

FLORIDA GARDEN
CASSEROLE

*4 servings*

*3 cups fresh tomatoes, cut into wedges*

*1 cup Cheddar cheese, shredded*

*1 1/4 cups herb-seasoned dry bread crumbs*

*1 1/4 cup green pepper, chopped*

*1 small onion, diced*

*1/4 cup margarine, melted*

*1/4 teaspoon pepper*

*1/2 teaspoon salt*

*Preheat at 350° F. Combine tomatoes, cheese, bread crumbs, green pepper, onion, margarine, pepper and salt in a large bowl. Transfer mixture into a greased 1 1/2 quart baking dish. Bake 35 minutes or until vegetables are tender.*

MEADOWBROOK
GOLF COURSE

135

# SIDE DISHES

### MOROCCAN COUSCOUS AUX LEGUMES

*4 to 6 servings*

6 cups warm water

1 pound lamb or chicken, boneless, cut into bite-size pieces

1 medium onion, chopped

4 teaspoons olive oil

2 teaspoons salt

2 teaspoons pepper

pinch saffron

1/2 teaspoon turmeric

1/2 pound carrots, chopped

1 or 2 medium large turnips, chopped

1 cup cabbage, chopped

2 zucchini, sliced

2 medium tomatoes, chopped

8 ounces or 1 cup garbanzo beans

1 cup boiling water

1 cup couscous, uncooked

3/4 teaspoon salt

hot pepper sauce

136

Bring warm water to boil. Add lamb or chicken, onion, olive oil, salt, pepper, saffron and turmeric. Reduce heat and simmer one hour. Add carrots, turnips, cabbage, zucchini and tomatoes; continue cooking 30 to 40 minutes until vegetables are tender. Add garbanzo beans. Simmer another 10 minutes. This mixture should be a little watery. If it is not, add a little water to give it some broth. In another pot, bring one cup water to a boil; add couscous and salt. Stir and cover. Remove from heat and let sit 20 minutes or until couscous has absorbed all the water and is tender. Toss the couscous with 1/2 to 3/4 cup of the sauce from the vegetable mixture.

To serve, place 1 cup couscous on plate and place vegetable mixture in the center of couscous. Sprinkle with more vegetable sauce, if desired. Pass hot pepper sauce for those who want a little extra kick.

## BASIL TOMATO TART

*8 servings*

9-inch pastry shell, uncooked

1 1/2 cups Mozzarella cheese, grated

5 to 6 plum tomatoes, sliced into 8 slices
each, seeded

1 cup fresh basil leaves

4 garlic cloves

1/2 cup mayonnaise

1/4 cup Parmesan cheese

1/8 teaspoon pepper

Preheat oven to 450° F. Line pastry shell with aluminum foil and bake for 5 minutes. Remove foil and bake for an additional 8 minutes. Remove pastry shell from oven and sprinkle with 1/2 cup Mozzarella cheese. Reduce oven temperature to 375° F. Arrange tomatoes over pastry crust. In a food processor, chop basil and garlic. Sprinkle over tomatoes. Combine mayonnaise, Parmesan cheese, pepper and 1 cup Mozzarella cheese. Spoon over pastry crust. Bake 20 minutes.

## HERBED ORZO

*Chef Steve Williams, Steve's Café Americain*

*6 servings*

3 tablespoons olive oil

2 shallots, minced

1 tablespoon garlic, minced

6 mushrooms, sliced

1 tomato, diced

1/4 cup mixed herbs (primarily basil with
  oregano, thyme, rosemary, or other
  favorite herbs added)

16 ounces orzo, cooked, cooled, tossed with
  1 tablespoon oil

1/3 cup dry white wine

salt and pepper to taste

Heat the olive oil in a large sauté pan. Add
the shallots, garlic and mushrooms. Cook 3
minutes. Add the tomatoes, cook for a
minute longer. Add the mixed
herbs and the orzo. Mix well.
Stir in wine and salt and
pepper to taste. Serve hot.

## STUFFED SQUASH

*2 to 4 servings*

2 medium to large yellow squash

8 saltine crackers, crushed coarse

1/4 teaspoon garlic powder

1 tablespoon butter, softened

1/3 cup sharp Cheddar cheese, grated

salt and pepper, to taste

Cover whole squash with water and bring to a boil. Boil until just tender. Remove squash from water immediately. Cut squash in half, lengthwise. In medium bowl combine crackers, garlic powder, butter, Cheddar cheese, salt and pepper. When squash is cool enough to handle, scoop out centers of each half and mix with other ingredients. (If very moist add a few more saltines.) Fill the squash with stuffing and place on cookie sheet, stuffing side up. Just before serving, brown squash under the broiler. They should be crispy and dark golden in color.

## OKRA PILÂU
*4 servings*

2 cups okra, sliced thin

3 slices bacon, diced

2 teaspoons oil or butter

1/2 cup green pepper, chopped

1/4 cup onion, chopped

1 cup white rice, uncooked

2 cups chicken broth

1 16-ounce can tomatoes, drained and
chopped

1 teaspoon salt

Sauté okra and bacon in oil or butter in a
large skillet. Add green peppers, onions, rice,
chicken broth, tomatoes and salt. Bring to
a boil and cover. Reduce heat and simmer
15 to 20 minutes. Fluff with fork.

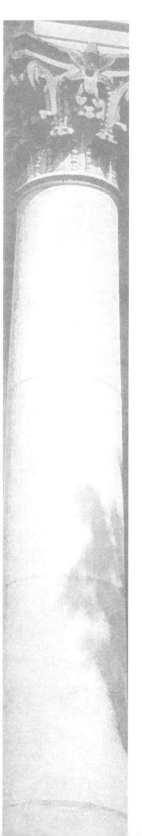

# SIDE DISHES

### SMASHED POTATOES
(EASY AND LOWFAT)
*10 servings*

10 whole small red potatoes, unpeeled
water
8 servings instant mashed potatoes,
    prepared according to directions
    substituting fat-free margarine
6 ounces fat-free cream cheese
8 ounces fat-free sour cream
1/2 red onion, chopped and sautéed
salt and pepper to taste
dash of paprika
chopped chives, optional

In large pot place potatoes, add water to cover. Bring to a boil, reduce heat and cook gently until potatoes are tender. With potato masher, lightly crush potatoes, but do not mash completely (there should be small chunks). Set aside. Combine instant potatoes and cream cheese until smooth, then add sour cream and mix thoroughly. Stir in onions. In a large bowl, combine both potatoes and add salt and pepper to taste. Garnish with paprika and fresh chives, if desired.

For buffet: Prepare as above and spoon into lightly-greased baking dish. Brush top with 1 tablespoon melted butter or dot with butter (can use fat-free). Bake immediately or cover and refrigerate. If refrigerated, let stand at room temperature for 30 minutes before baking. Bake at 350° F, uncovered 30 minutes or until hot.

142

## TANGY ASPARAGUS

*6 servings*

1 1/2 pounds asparagus

2 tablespoons butter

1/2 cup bread crumbs

1/8 teaspoon garlic salt

1/8 teaspoon pepper

8 ounces sour cream

2 tablespoons prepared horseradish

bread crumbs for topping

Preheat oven to 350° F. Cut ends off asparagus and steam 7 to 10 minutes. Melt butter, add bread crumbs, garlic salt and pepper. Stir until brown. Place asparagus in a 8 x 12-inch baking dish. Combine sour cream and horseradish and pour over asparagus. Top with bread crumbs. Bake 8 to 10 minutes.

### SUPERB HERBS

*You can enhance the flavor of many dishes by adding fresh herbs. Whether you pick them yourself or purchase them, use herbs on the same day or refrigerate them. Herbs should be kept dry, with the exception of basil, cilantro and parsley, which can be placed in a container with a little water. Use a resealable plastic bag for storing fresh herbs in the refrigerator.*

*Be careful not to overdo it when adding herbs. You can always add more. Dried herbs have a highly concentrated flavor. It only takes one teaspoon of dried herbs to equal the flavor of one tablespoon of fresh herbs.*

*Fresh herbs also make fantastic garnishes and add a special "gourmet" touch.*

*Delicious ways to use herbs are throughout this cookbook. Try some of the following suggestions...*

*For delicate herbs like parsley, chives or chervil, Lemon Chive Pasta page 166*

*For medium herbs like dill, thyme or marjoram Parmesan Scalloped Potatoes page 128*

*For accent herbs like oregano, basil, tarragon or coriander, Basil Tomato Tart page 138*

*For strong herbs like sage, bay or rosemary, Simon and Garfunkel Chicken page 170*

ROBINSHORE, INC.

## BROCCOLI STUFFED TOMATOES

*8 servings*

6 medium tomatoes

salt and pepper to taste

1 10-ounce package frozen chopped broccoli (cooked according to package directions) or 2 1/2 cups fresh broccoli, steamed until tender-crisp

1 cup Swiss cheese, shredded

1 cup soft bread crumbs

1/3 cup mayonnaise

1 garlic clove, minced

2 tablespoons onion, chopped

2 tablespoons fresh Parmesan cheese, grated

Preheat oven to 350° F. Cut tops off tomatoes. Scoop out pulp and seeds leaving shells intact. Sprinkle insides of tomatoes with salt and pepper; invert for 30 minutes to drain. Drain cooked or steamed broccoli and combine with Swiss cheese, bread crumbs, mayonnaise, garlic and onion. Stuff tomatoes with cheese and broccoli mixture. Place in shallow baking dish and sprinkle with Parmesan cheese. Bake 30 minutes.

Entrees

## The Thomas Center

Life was grand at the Thomas Center. Surrounded by lush gardens, the restored Mediterranean Revival/Italian Renaissance style building was once the home of the family of Major William Reuben Thomas. Major Thomas, a former state senator and Gainesville mayor, was instrumental in the selection of Gainesville as the site of the University of Florida. The building continued as a personal residence until 1926, when it became part of the Hotel Thomas. For 40 years, it offered guest rooms to area visitors.

In 1973, the building was listed on the National Registry of Historic Places and became the Thomas Center. The Junior League of Gainesville aided in the refurbishing of Period Rooms as part of the overall restoration of this historic building. The 1920s Period Rooms provide a glimpse of the original interiors and decorating trends of the day and reflect the affluent lifestyle of the Thomas family.

This Gainesville landmark provides the community with a beautiful place for art exhibits, concerts and local history exhibits. The restored gardens surrounding the Thomas Center provide a lovely setting to enjoy a sunny afternoon.

THE PRECEDING PAGE PRESENTED BY CLARK & DEBORAH BUTLER—BUTLER PLAZA, THE MIRACLE MILE, SARAH AND REED BROWN, ERIC W. SCOTT, MD/dba FLORIDA NEUROSURGICAL ASSOCIATES

# ENTREES

## SAVORY MARINADE

1 1/2 cups salad oil
3/4 cup soy sauce
1/4 cup Worcestershire sauce
2 tablespoons dry mustard
1 tablespoon pepper
1/2 cup wine vinegar
1 1/2 teaspoons dried parsley
2 1/2 teaspoons salt
1/3 cup lemon juice
garlic salt to taste

Combine all ingredients. Marinate roast or tenderloin 3 to 4 hours or overnight. Grill or bake, basting with the marinade. This marinade is delicious with chicken, beef, pork or fish.

## MUSTARD SAUCE

1 cup brown sugar, light
1/3 cup dry mustard
1 heaping tablespoon flour
1/2 cup vinegar
1/2 cup warm water
1 beef bouillon cube
2 eggs, beaten

Dissolve 1 beef bouillon cube in 1/2 cup warm water. Add brown sugar, mustard, flour, vinegar mixing well. Stir in the 2 eggs. Cook over low heat, stirring constantly, do not boil, cook until thickened.

This is great for a party and goes well with beef, turkey and ham.

# SWEDISH MEATBALLS

*6 servings*

1 pound ground beef

1/2 pound fresh ground pork

1/3 cup onion, minced

3/4 cup soft bread crumbs

3 tablespoons parsley, chopped

1/2 teaspoon marjoram

1 teaspoon salt

1 teaspoon Worcestershire sauce

1 egg

1/3 cup milk

1/2 cup shortening

1/4 cup flour

1 teaspoon paprika

2 cups beef bouillon, hot

3/4 cup sour cream

Combine ground beef, ground pork, onion, bread crumbs, parsley, marjoram, salt, Worcestershire sauce, egg and milk. Mix well. Shape into 1 1/2-inch balls. Brown in shortening. Remove from pan. Blend flour with drippings in pan. Add paprika; then slowly add hot beef bouillon. Cook, stirring until thickened and smooth. Lower heat; stir in sour cream. Return meatballs to pan and heat thoroughly.

149

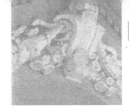

### GROUND BEEF WITH TOMATO (PICADILLO)

*4 servings*

1 pound ground beef

1 8-ounce can tomato sauce

1 medium onion, diced

1 green pepper, diced

3 garlic cloves, minced

1 whole tomato, diced

1 tablespoon ground oregano

1 1/2 teaspoons ground cumin

1 tablespoon garlic powder

salt and pepper to taste

1/4 cup raisins

1 teaspoon hot sauce

Combine all ingredients in a Dutch oven; cover and cook over medium heat until meat is cooked and liquids are absorbed. Serve over white rice.

# DRUNKEN BEEF TENDERLOIN

*8 to 10 servings*

2 cups bourbon

1 garlic clove, minced

2 tablespoons lemon juice

1 tablespoon sugar

1 teaspoon salt

3 whole cloves

1 teaspoon dry mustard

1/2 teaspoon ground ginger

2 tablespoons Worcestershire sauce

4 tablespoons orange marmalade

1 3 to 4-pound beef tenderloin, center cut, trimmed

1/2 cup olive oil

fresh ground pepper for rub

Preheat oven to 425° F. Combine bourbon, garlic, lemon juice, sugar, salt, cloves, mustard, ginger, Worcestershire sauce and marmalade; heat in a saucepan. DO NOT BOIL. Remove from heat and let cool completely. Place beef tenderloin in ziplock bag and add marinade. Close and marinate 18 to 24 hours. Heat olive oil in skillet. Remove tenderloin from the marinade and rub with fresh ground pepper. Brown on all sides in oil. Remove from the skillet and place on a well-oiled rack in a roasting pan. Pour 1/2 cup of the marinade over the beef. Roast until meat thermometer registers 125° F for rare or 140° F for medium. Let stand 10 minutes before carving.

### DOWN SOUTH BARBECUE

*10 to 12 servings*

1 1/2 pounds chuck roast, cubed

1 1/2 pounds pork, cubed

1 6-ounce can tomato paste

1/2 cup brown sugar

1/4 cup cider vinegar

2 tablespoons chili powder

2 teaspoons salt

1 teaspoon dry mustard

2 teaspoons Worcestershire sauce

1 cup water

Combine all ingredients in a Dutch oven. Bring to boil and simmer covered for 3 hours. Stir cooked mixture with a wire whisk until shredded. Serve on hamburger buns or round hard rolls.

 **Tip**
*Can also be cooked in a slow cooker on high (300° F) for 8 hours. Omit water if using this method.*

152

## Veal Scallopini Con Cognac

*4 servings*

1 pound veal scallopini
flour for dredging
3 tablespoons olive oil, preferably flavored
1 large clove garlic, minced
8 ounces mushrooms, sliced
4 green onions, chopped with green portion
4 plum tomatoes, sliced
1 cube beef bouillon
1/2 cup hot water
3 ounces cognac, preferably Courvoisier
2 tablespoons fresh marjoram, chopped
salt and pepper to taste
fresh chopped parsley
cooked pasta
fresh Parmesan cheese, grated

Pound veal flat and dredge in flour. Heat 1 1/2 tablespoons olive oil in skillet. Cook veal over medium-high heat 45 seconds per side. Remove and place on paper towel. Heat remainder of oil, add garlic, mushrooms and green onions. Sauté 3 minutes over medium-high heat stirring frequently. Add tomatoes and sauté 2 more minutes. Dissolve bouillon in water. Deglaze pan with cognac. Add bouillon, marjoram, salt and pepper. Cook 2 minutes and stirring constantly, sift 1/2 tablespoon flour over top; mix well. Return veal and simmer until thickened. Place over pasta, top with parsley and Parmesan cheese.

153

### Brunswick Stew

*8 to 10 quarts*

4 pound stewing hen

4 pound pork roast

Salt and boil separately the hen and pork roast until well done. Drain, reserving some broth if desired, to make stew thinner. Cool meats and chip or shred the meats and set aside. Refrigerate if stew will be made the following day.

2 32-ounce cans crushed tomatoes

3 medium onions, chopped fine

2 17-ounce cans creamed corn

6 to 8 chicken bouillon cubes

Combine and cook tomatoes, onions and corn in a large pot, uncovered at medium temperature for 30 minutes. Add bouillon cubes.

Reduce Heat to Simmer and Add:

chipped meats (from above)

1 26-ounce bottle ketchup

1 cup apple cider vinegar or sweet pickle juice

1 5-ounce bottle Worcestershire sauce

juice of 3 lemons

1 tablespoon hot pepper sauce, to taste

1 tablespoon black pepper

1 11-ounce can shoe peg corn

1 10-ounce bottle steak sauce

1 teaspoon crushed red pepper

salt and pepper to taste


Simmer uncovered, one hour.


*Note:*
*This recipe freezes well and can be halved easily.*

155

## CARNITAS WITH SALSA ASADA

*Serves 8*

Carnitas:

3 pounds pork tenderloin,
   cut into 1-inch cubes

4 garlic cloves, halved

1 large onion, halved

2 ribs celery, quartered

3 14-ounce cans ( 5 1/2 cups) chicken broth

salt to taste

2 tablespoons olive oil

1 large onion, chopped

1 bunch cilantro leaves, chopped

In a large pot or Dutch oven, combine pork cubes, garlic, onion, celery and broth. Bring to a boil over high heat. Cover and reduce heat to low. Cook 1 hour or until meat is tender. Add water during cooking to keep meat covered. Salt to taste. Remove meat; broth may be saved for another use.

In a large skillet, heat oil over medium-high heat. Add pork cubes and sauté, stirring occasionally for 5 to 8 minutes or until pork is brown and crisp on the outside. Drain on paper towels, then transfer meat to serving platter. Sprinkle with chopped onion and cilantro.

## Salsa Asada:

5 medium ripe tomatoes

2 fresh jalapeno peppers

5 sprigs cilantro leaves

1 tablespoon onion, chopped

Salt to taste

Preheat broiler to 550° F with rack positioned six inches from the broiler. Place tomatoes and jalapenos in a greased 9 x 13-inch baking pan. Broil seven minutes per side, turning once, or until skins are charred and cracked.

Transfer tomatoes and peppers to a plate and cool for 15 minutes. Peel skins, reserving some charred pieces. CAUTION: be careful to use rubber gloves and/or wash hands after handling peppers. Discard the rest of the skins.

Roughly chop tomatoes and peppers and place in a food processor fitted with a metal blade. Add reserved charred skins, cilantro, and onion. Process into small pieces. Do not purée. Add salt to taste. Serve carnitas rolled into a warm tortilla with salsa asada. Great with black beans.

## CROWN ROAST OF PORK

*10 to 12 servings*

2 pork loins, center cut, no less than 8 pounds

At least one chop per person. Have butcher tie the loins together to form a crown and trim the meat back from the rib end points.

1 tablespoon dried marjoram

1 tablespoon dried rosemary

Salt and pepper to taste

Preheat oven to 325° F. Combine marjoram, rosemary, salt and pepper; rub mixture all over roast. Cover points with aluminum foil to prevent them from burning during roasting. Place crown roast in roasting pan; insert meat thermometer and cook uncovered, basting often with pan juices. When the pork reaches 130° F, 1 1/2 to 2 1/2 hours, fill the cavity with dressing.

## Apple and Raisin Dressing:

1/2 cup of butter

6 tablespoons water

1 cup celery, chopped

1 cup onions, chopped

4 cups bread crumbs, freshly toasted

3 cups Granny Smith apples, peeled and chopped

1/2 cup golden raisins

1 teaspoon baking powder

1 tablespoon dried rosemary

salt and pepper to taste

Melt butter with water in a large skillet, add celery and onions. Sauté until onions have absorbed butter and are limp. Do not brown. Add bread crumbs, apples, raisins, baking powder and rosemary. Toss well. Stuffing should be loose.

Make a collar with aluminum foil, place it beside the crown and fill with extra stuffing. Pork is thoroughly cooked at 170° F. The rule for cooking pork is 30 minutes per pound, this may be too much, so use a meat thermometer. Increase the oven temperature to 425° F during the final minutes of cooking to get a toasted effect.

159

RICHARD W. OLIVER, JR. DMD, PA

# ENTREES

## CABIN RIBS
*6 to 8 servings*

*Marinade:*
1/2 cup tequila
1/2 cup coffee flavored liqueur
1 tablespoon red pepper flakes
1 tablespoon thyme
1 lime chopped with juice

*Sauce:*
3/4 cup chili sauce
juice of 1 lime
1 teaspoon liquid smoke
1 tablespoon Worcestershire sauce
freshly ground pepper
1 tablespoon hot pepper sauce
1/2 cup marinade
1 1/2 teaspoons brown sugar

3 pounds baby back ribs

Prepare marinade in blender and pour over rib slabs in glass dish. Cover and refrigerate for at least 3 hours, turning often. In a pitcher combine sauce ingredients with 1/2 cup of reserved marinade. Grill ribs over semi-hot coals after brushing with the sauce. Continue to turn the ribs while brushing on the sauce, cooling slowly until done. Be patient they're worth it!

## BARBECUE BRISKET
*10 to 12 servings*

1 tablespoon ground pepper

3 to 4 pound beef brisket

1 teaspoon onion salt

1 teaspoon garlic salt

2 tablespoons liquid smoke

1 1/2 teaspoons Worcestershire sauce

1 cup barbecue sauce

Pepper brisket well. Mix onion salt, garlic salt, liquid smoke, and Worcestershire sauce together and cover both sides of brisket well. Place brisket in baking dish and pierce in several places with a fork. Pour barbecue sauce over the brisket, cover and place in the refrigerator overnight. Bake at 250° F for 5 to 7 hours while covered. The last hour you may want to uncover and baste frequently. When done, slice against grain.

161

## BOLICHI
*6 to 8 servings*

1/2 pound ground beef (or beef, chopped fine —cut from pocket inside of roast)

1 chorizo sausage, minced

1 medium onion, minced

1/4 cup green pepper, chopped

1/2 cup olives, chopped

1 tablespoon Worcestershire sauce

1/2 cup ketchup

flour to coat roast

Eye of round roast (with pocket cut the length of the round, but open at only one end)

1/4 teaspoon garlic salt

1/2 teaspoon fresh ground pepper

1 15-ounce can beef broth

Preheat oven to 475° F. Combine ground beef, sausage, onion, green pepper, olives, Worcestershire sauce and ketchup. Mix ingredients thoroughly. Fill pocket cut into roast with stuffing. Be sure that it is completely filled; force to end of pocket. Cover surface of roast with flour and place uncovered in a roasting pan in a hot oven 15 to 18 minutes. Remove roast from oven, sprinkle with garlic salt and pepper. Pour beef broth over roast and return to oven. Roast, uncovered for two hours at 325° F. Baste frequently with broth. Remove from oven, place on hot platter and slice into thin portions with electric knife. Serve with yellow rice.

## SPAGHETTI SAUCE

*6 to 8 servings*

2 medium onions, chopped
1 green pepper, chopped
3 garlic cloves, chopped
1/4 cup olive oil
2 14-ounce cans Italian tomatoes
1 12-ounce can tomato paste
1 12-ounce can tomato sauce
1 teaspoon salt
1 teaspoon dried basil
1 teaspoon sugar
2 tablespoons parsley, chopped fine
1/2 teaspoon oregano
1/4 teaspoon black pepper
1 cup red wine
1/2 pound hot Italian sausage
1 pound ground chuck
8 ounces fresh mushrooms, sliced

In medium skillet sauté onions, green pepper and garlic in olive oil. In slow-cooker or Dutch oven combine sautéed mixture with tomatoes, tomato paste, tomato sauce, salt, basil, sugar, parsley, oregano, pepper and wine. Stir together, cover and cook over low heat 2 hours. Brown sausage and ground chuck, drain and add to sauce along with mushrooms. Cook covered over low heat 1 to 2 more hours.

# ENTREES

## MEXICAN LASAGNA
*8 servings*

2 cups onion, chopped

1 1/2 cups green pepper, chopped

1 14-ounce can tomatoes, undrained and cut

3/4 cup picante sauce

2 garlic cloves, chopped

2 teaspoons cumin

2 15-ounce cans black beans, drained

12 6-inch tortillas

2 cups Monterey Jack cheese, shredded

Preheat oven to 350° F. In a large skillet combine onion, green pepper, tomatoes, picante sauce, garlic and cumin. Bring to a boil. Reduce heat and simmer uncovered for 10 minutes. Stir in drained beans. Spread one third of the bean mixture on bottom of 9 x 13-inch baking pan. Top with half of the tortillas and half of the cheese. Layer one third of the bean mixture, tortillas, remaining bean mixture and cheese. Cover and bake 30 to 35 minutes. Let stand for 10 minutes before cutting.

 *Idea!*

*Garnish with chopped tomatoes, lettuce, green onions, black olives and sour cream, if desired.*

## TOMATO-OLIVE TWO-CHEESE PASTA

*8 servings*

1 1/2 cups onion, chopped
1 teaspoon garlic, minced
3 tablespoons olive oil
3 28-ounce cans Italian plum tomatoes
2 10 1/2-ounce cans low-salt chicken broth
2 teaspoons dried basil
1 teaspoon dried crushed red pepper
1 pound penne or rigatoni pasta
3 tablespoons olive oil
8 ounces Havarti cheese, grated
1/3 cup Kalamata olives, pitted and sliced
1/3 cup Parmesan cheese, grated
1/4 cup fresh basil, chopped fine
salt and pepper to taste

Sauté onion and garlic in olive oil in a heavy Dutch oven over medium-high heat until translucent (5 to 6 minutes). Stir in tomatoes, broth, basil and red pepper. Break up tomatoes with a spoon as they cook. Bring mixture to a boil and reduce heat to medium-low. Simmer for 1 1/2 hours. Season with salt and pepper. Preheat oven to 375° F. Cook pasta according to package directions. Drain well and toss with 3 table-spoons of olive oil. Combine pasta, tomato sauce and Havarti cheese. Mix well and spoon into a 9 x 13-inch baking dish and sprinkle with olives and Parmesan cheese. Bake 30 minutes. Sprinkle with basil before serving.

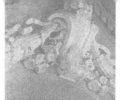
## LEMON CHIVE PASTA
*4 servings*

2 tablespoons unsalted butter

1 tablespoon fresh chives, chopped

2 tablespoons olive oil, divided

zest of 1/2 lemon, grated

8 ounces pasta (linguini, spaghetti or
fettucine)

salt and pepper to taste

Melt butter and sauté chives lightly 1 to 2
minutes over medium heat. Add 1 tablespoon
of the olive oil and lemon zest and sauté
1 minute. Do not let mixture brown.

Cook the pasta in large pot of boiling water
until al denté. Drain well and toss with
remaining tablespoon of olive oil and chive
mixture. Season with salt and pepper to
taste. Serve immediately.

## PASTA SAUCE— FLORIDA STYLE

*6 servings*

2 garlic cloves, minced

1 onion, chopped

3 stalks celery, chopped

2 tablespoons olive oil

1/4 teaspoon thyme

1/4 teaspoon basil

1/2 teaspoon oregano

1/2 teaspoon salt

2 14.5-ounce cans diced tomatoes

2 6-ounce cans tomato paste

1/2 cup dry white wine

2 8-ounce bottles clam juice

4 4.5-ounce cans minced clams, drained

1 pound boiled shrimp, shelled

1/2 cup parsley, chopped

Sauté garlic, onion and celery in oil. Add thyme, basil, oregano, salt, tomatoes, tomato paste and wine. Simmer uncovered 1 hour. Add clam juice and continue to simmer 30 minutes. Add clams and shrimp and simmer an additional 10 minutes. Serve over favorite pasta.

167

## CHICKEN TARRAGON

*4 servings*

4 boneless, skinless chicken breasts

1/4 teaspoon salt

1/4 teaspoon black pepper

1 tablespoon olive oil

1 pound fresh asparagus, cut into 1-inch pieces

1 small red bell pepper, cut into thin strips

1/4 cup white wine

1 tablespoon tarragon, dried

3 cups cooked white rice, made using 1 cup chicken broth, 1 cup water and 1 cup rice

Preheat oven to 350° F. Season chicken with salt and pepper. Bake in a covered dish until done. Cut into strips. Heat olive oil in a large skillet, add asparagus and red pepper. Sauté until tender-crisp then add wine and tarragon. Simmer 2 minutes. Serve asparagus mixture over cooked rice and top with chicken strips.

## PARTY CHICKEN

*8 servings*

salt and pepper to taste

4 whole chicken breasts, split

1 tablespoon Italian dressing mix

1/4 cup butter, melted

1 can cream of mushroom soup

1 4-ounce package whipped cream cheese with chives

1/3 cup Sauterne, may use other white wine

parsley, for garnish

rice

Preheat oven to 325° F. Salt and pepper chicken, sprinkle with dressing mix and brown slowly in melted butter. Place in baking dish. Blend soup, cream cheese and add Sauterne. Spoon over chicken. Baste once or twice during baking. Garnish with parsley and serve with rice. Bake uncovered for 1 hour.

## SIMON AND
## GARFUNKEL CHICKEN

*4 servings*

1 4 1/2-pound roaster chicken

Kosher salt

2 teaspoons dried rosemary, crumbled

1 1/2 teaspoons ground or rubbed sage

1 1/2 teaspoons dried thyme

fresh ground pepper

2 bay leaves

5 tablespoons olive oil

4 small russet potatoes, unpeeled,
    quartered lengthwise and cut crosswise
    into 1/2-inch pieces

8 large shallots, peeled

Preheat oven to 425° F. Rub chicken inside and out with salt. Combine rosemary, sage, thyme and generous amount of pepper in small bowl. Rub some of the mixture inside the chicken. Place 1 bay leaf in cavity of chicken. Tie legs together to hold shape. Brush with olive oil. Sprinkle with half of remaining herb mixture. Place in large baking dish. Surround with potatoes and shallots. Sprinkle vegetables with remaining herb mixture and olive oil. Add bay leaf and mix well.

Baste chicken with pan juices and turn vegetables occasionally. Roast chicken until juices run clear when pierced in thickest part of the thigh, about 1 hour and 15 minutes. Transfer chicken to platter. Using slotted spoon, place vegetables around the chicken. Tent with aluminum foil to keep warm while preparing the sauce.

Sauce:

1 3/4 cups chicken stock

1/4 cup balsamic vinegar

3 tablespoons unsalted butter,
   cut into pieces

fresh parsley, minced

171

Pour pan juices into glass measuring cup and degrease. Add enough stock to measure 2 cups. Add vinegar to baking pan and bring to boil over medium heat, scraping up any browned bits. Boil until reduced to glaze, about 4 minutes. Add stock mixture and boil until reduced to 1 cup, about 6 minutes. Reduce heat and whisk in butter, 1 piece at a time. Adjust seasoning to taste. Stir in parsley. Pour sauce over chicken and vegetables and serve.

# ENTREES

## SPINACH STUFFED CHICKEN BREASTS

*6 servings*

1 1/2 tablespoons light margarine

6 ounces fresh mushrooms, chopped fine

1 10-ounce package frozen, chopped spinach,
thawed and drained

1 8-ounce package low fat cream cheese,
at room temperature

1/2 cup fresh chives, chopped
(can substitute green onions)

salt and pepper to taste

6 chicken breast halves with skin

6 tablespoons Dijon mustard

Preheat oven to 450° F. Melt margarine in skillet over medium heat. Add mushrooms and sauté until tender, about 5 minutes. In a large bowl, blend spinach, cream cheese and chives. Stir mushrooms into spinach mixture and season with salt and pepper.

Wash chicken and loosen skin to create a pocket for the spinach mixture. Divide spinach mixture into 6 portions and stuff into each chicken breast. Arrange chicken breasts on a baking sheet and spread each with 1 tablespoon of Dijon mustard.

Bake chicken until golden brown and fully cooked, approximately 25 minutes. Can be made ahead and frozen.

## CHICKEN ARTICHOKE

*6 servings*

9 chicken pieces (breasts and/or thighs)

salt

pepper and paprika to taste

6 tablespoons butter, divided

12 artichoke hearts or 1 15-ounce can

1/4 pound mushrooms, cut into large pieces

2 tablespoons flour

1 cup chicken bouillon

3 tablespoons sherry

Preheat oven to 375° F. Generously sprinkle salt, pepper and paprika on chicken. Brown chicken in 4 tablespoons butter and place in large, shallow casserole. Arrange artichoke hearts around chicken pieces. Add 2 tablespoons butter to frying pan and sauté mushrooms for 5 minutes. Sprinkle flour over frying pan mixture and stir in chicken bouillon. When smooth and thickened to nice consistency, add sherry. If serving within hour, pour over chicken and bake 40 minutes. If preparing ahead, stop, and cover chicken to prevent drying. When ready to cook, uncover, pour sauce over chicken and bake.

173

## CHICKEN BASQUE
*6 to 8 servings*

1 1/2 pounds boneless, skinless chicken breasts cut into 1-inch cubes

1 cup flour

2 tablespoons olive oil

2 pounds zucchini, cut in 3/4 inch rounds

salt and pepper to taste

3/4 pound whole Italian sausage

1 tablespoon butter

1 garlic clove, minced

1/2 pound mushrooms, if small, add whole; if large, quartered

1 medium onion, chopped

1/4 cup olive oil

1 cup vermouth

12 ounces roasted peppers, chopped

1 tablespoon parsley

1 crumbled bay leaf

1/2 teaspoon basil

1/2 teaspoon thyme

Coat chicken in flour and set aside. Place large skillet over high heat and add 2 tablespoons olive oil. When hot, add zucchini. Saute 3 minutes or until nicely browned. Season with salt and pepper, remove with slotted spoon; set aside. Add whole sausage and saute over medium heat until brown. Slice sausage into 1/2-inch slices and set aside. Skim off all but 1 tablespoon of fat and add butter, garlic, mushrooms and onions; cook until wilted and remove with slotted spoon. Saute chicken in 1/4 cup olive oil, and cook over medium to high heat, until browned and done. Add vermouth, sausage, roasted peppers, reserved vegetables and herbs; heat through and simmer 5 minutes. Can be made ahead and refrigerated or frozen.

 *Idea!*

*Put the whole sausage in a microwave-safe dish and cook about 45 seconds, remove sausage and blot with paper towels (this removes more grease and assures that the sausage is thoroughly cooked).*

175

### CHICKEN STUFFED SHELLS WITH SPINACH BÉCHAMEL SAUCE

*4 servings*

12 large seashell shaped pasta

Cook the pasta shells in plenty of boiling salted water until barely cooked, about 7 minutes; drain. Let stand in a bowl of cool water until ready to use.

Filling:

3 tablespoons butter

3 teaspoons shallots, chopped fine

1 cup mushrooms, chopped

3 slices proscuitto, chopped fine

2 cups cooked chicken, shredded

2 tablespoons parsley, chopped

15 ounces Ricotta cheese

1 egg, beaten

1/4 cup Parmesan cheese, grated

For the filling, heat the butter in a medium skillet; add the shallots and mushrooms; sautè until tender, about 10 minutes. Add the proscuitto; saute 2 minutes. Stir in the chicken and parsley. In a large bowl, combine the Ricotta, egg, and Parmesan cheese; fold in chicken mixture until blended. Set aside.

**Sauce:**

3 tablespoons butter

3 teaspoons all purpose flour

2 cups milk, heated

10 ounces frozen chopped spinach, drained and squeezed dry

1 teaspoon fresh lemon juice

1 teaspoon salt

pinch of nutmeg

freshly ground pepper

1/4 cup Parmesan cheese, grated, for topping

For the sauce, heat the butter in a small saucepan, gradually stir in flour. Cook stirring constantly, until smooth, about 3 minutes. Gradually stir in milk and cook stirring constantly until smooth and thickened, about 10 minutes. Purée the spinach with half of the bechamel in a food processor or blender. Add the remaining bechamel and lemon juice. Season with salt, nutmeg, and pepper. Set aside.

Preheat oven to 350° F. Lightly butter a 9 x 13-inch baking dish. Drain the pasta and invert on paper towels to blot dry. Fill shells with the chicken mixture. Arrange in baking dish. Pour the bechamel over the top. Sprinkle with some Parmesan.

Cover with foil and bake 30 minutes. Uncover and bake until browned and bubbly, about 15 minutes. Let stand approximately 10 minutes before serving.

Can be made ahead.

# ENTREES

## SPICY CHICKEN FINGERS

1 tablespoon salt

3/4 teaspoon garlic powder

1/2 teaspoon onion powder

3/4 teaspoon black pepper

1/2 teaspoon white pepper

1/2 teaspoon ground cumin

1/4 teaspoon ground red pepper flakes

1/2 teaspoon paprika

4 boneless, skinless chicken breasts, with all
visible fat removed, sliced into 1-inch strips

olive oil

In a small bowl mix the salt, garlic powder, onion powder, peppers, cumin, red pepper flakes and paprika together. Set aside. In a medium bowl with a lid, or resealable plastic bag, combine chicken and olive oil. Coat chicken thoroughly with the oil. Sprinkle the spice mixture on the chicken. Roll the chicken around so each piece is fully coated. Cover chicken and marinate in the refrigerator for minimum of an hour. Preheat a dry griddle or frying pan over medium high heat. Place the chicken in the hot pan. Do not add any extra oil. Cook chicken approximately 4 minutes per side. Remove from heat. Serve chicken strips with Blue cheese dressing for dipping, if desired.

## Mediterranean Chicken

1/2 cup olive oil

4 boneless and skinless, chicken breasts,
   sliced into 1-inch strips with all fat removed

2 ounces dry white wine

1 1/2 ounces white wine vinegar

4 tablespoons butter

2 garlic cloves, minced

1/2 teaspoon rosemary

1 1/2 tablespoons capers, drained

5 anchovy fillets, chopped fine

4 tablespoons parsley, chopped

1/2 teaspoon crushed red pepper flakes

Heat the olive oil over medium heat in a large skillet. Sautè the chicken strips in oil until tender. Add remaining ingredients and mix well. Cover the skillet and cook over low heat for 25 to 30 minutes. Serve over white rice.

# ENTREES

### CHICKEN WITH RED WINE VINEGAR AND GARLIC
*Serves 4 to 6*

1/3 cup olive oil
1 frying chicken, cut up
1/2 cup all purpose flour
salt and pepper
20 garlic cloves, peeled
2 fresh sprigs rosemary
1/2 cup red wine vinegar
1/2 cup chicken broth

In a heavy cast iron pot with a tight lid, heat olive oil. Lightly dust chicken with flour, salt and pepper and lightly brown, stirring often. Add garlic, rosemary, vinegar and chicken broth. Lower heat, cover and let simmer for 40 to 50 minutes. Arrange chicken on individual plates or serving platter. Pour pan juices over chicken. Serve with roasted potatoes, bread and a green salad.

## SMOTHERED QUAIL
*6 Servings*

6 quail
3/4 cup butter
1/4 cup water
1/2 cup flour
2 teaspoons garlic salt
1/2 teaspoon nutmeg
salt and pepper to taste
1/3 cup sherry

Preheat oven to 350° F. Brown quail on all sides in butter melted in a large skillet. After quail becomes brown, remove from pan. Add water to skillet and simmer to remove drippings from sides of pan. Add flour and mix forming a gravy. Stir in seasonings and sherry last. Place quail in baking dish and top with gravy. Cover and cook 1 to 1 1/2 hours. Serve with wild rice.

181

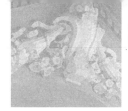

## CORNISH HEN WITH GRAPES
*4 Servings*

4 Cornish hens, giblets removed

salt and pepper

1/2 cup butter, cut in half

1/2 cup brandy

1/2 cup orange juice

1/3 cup red current jelly

2 tablespoons orange zest

1/4 teaspoon ground cloves

1/2 cup seedless green grapes, sliced

1/2 cup seedless red grapes, sliced

4 small bunches red grapes and more orange
    zest for garnish, if desired

182

Preheat oven to 350° F. Rub Cornish hens with salt and pepper. In a 5 quart oven-safe Dutch oven, melt 1/4 cup butter over medium heat. Add hens and sauté, turning occasionally until lightly browned, about 10 minutes. Cover and remove hens from heat and place in oven; roast 20 to 30 minutes. Transfer hens to platter. Over medium heat, add the remaining butter to drippings in dutch oven. Scrape browned bits from pan and blend in. Add brandy, orange juice, currant jelly, orange zest and cloves to pan; stir to melt jelly and blend sauce. Reduce heat to low and cook until sauce has thickened slightly and is darker in color, about 10 minutes. Add sliced green and red grapes to sauce. Return hens to Dutch oven and heat through. To serve, spoon some of the sauce onto each plate. Place one hen on individual plates; garnish with orange zest and one small bunch of red grapes, if desired.

# BASIL GRILLED CHICKEN
*serves 4*

3/4 teaspoon coarsely ground black pepper
4 boneless, skinless, chicken breast halves
1 cup butter or margarine, melted
1 cup fresh basil, chopped

Press 3/4 teaspoon pepper into meaty side of chicken breasts. Combine the butter and basil, stir well. Brush chicken lightly with melted butter mixture.

1 cup butter of margarine, softened, not
  melted
4 tablespoons fresh basil, minced
4 tablespoons Parmesan cheese, grated
1/2 teaspoon garlic powder
1/2 teaspoon salt
1/2 teaspoon pepper

garnish—fresh basil sprigs

Combine butter, basil, Parmesan cheese, garlic powder, salt and pepper in small bowl. Beat with electric mixer at low speed until smooth. Transfer to a small serving bowl; set aside.

Grill chicken over medium fire, basting with remaining melted butter mixture, 8 to 10 minutes on each side. Serve with the remaining basil and butter mixture. Spread desired amount on top of chicken. Garnish with basil sprigs.

## FAMILY BACKYARD MENU

*Southerners are known for their year-round grilling. If you've got an appetite for fun, be sure to include a family backyard grilled meal. It's an adventure for everyone when you dine outside. A little teamwork adds to the fun of the meal preparation; making memories is what it's all about. Have a backyard blast as you enjoy this menu.*

**Herb Garlic Bread**
*page 54*

**Lazy Day Lemonade**
*page 246*

**Black Bean and Rice Salad**
*page 112*

**Springtime Vegetable Salad**
*page 114*

**Baked Sweet Potatoes**
*page 132*

**Basil Grilled Chicken**
*page 183*

**Lime Meringue Pie**
*page 208*

STEVE'S CAFÈ AMERICAIN, INC.

183

### Salmon Pecan Bake

*4 servings*

4 salmon fillets (4 to 6 ounces each)

1/8 teaspoon salt

1/8 teaspoon pepper

2 tablespoons Dijon prepared mustard

2 tablespoons butter or margarine, melted

1 1/2 tablespoons honey

1/4 cup soft bread crumbs

1/4 cup pecans, chopped fine

2 teaspoons parsley, chopped

Fresh parsley sprigs and lemon slices
   for garnish

184

Preheat oven to 450° F. Sprinkle salmon with salt and pepper. Place fillets, skin side down, in lightly greased 9 x 13-inch baking dish. Combine mustard, butter and honey; brush on fillets. Combine bread crumbs, pecans and parsley. Spoon mixture evenly on top of each fillet. Bake fillets for 10 minutes or until flesh flakes easily when tested with a fork. Garnish if desired.

 *Idea!*

*This is an easy and elegant dish for guests. Pop it in while you're eating your first course. To save time, use commercial honey butter rather than separate ingredients. This dish is a wonderful alternative to salmon on the grill.*

## RED SNAPPER IN LOBSTER SAUCE

*4 servings*

4 tablespoons olive oil
4 7-ounce red snapper fillets
4 tablespoons flour

Preheat oven to 350° F. In a heavy skillet, heat olive oil. Dust snapper with flour and quickly sauté on both sides until lightly browned. Place in oven and cook an additional 8 to 10 minutes until fully cooked. Serve on warmed plates with lobster sauce.

Lobster Sauce:
4 ounces butter
2 garlic cloves, minced
4 tablespoons shallots, chopped
1/8 cup sweet vermouth
1 cup chicken broth
1 cup tomato juice
1/4 cup lobster or crab meat, cooked and
    chopped
salt and pepper to taste

In a medium skillet, melt butter, add garlic and shallots. Sauté 3 to 4 minutes over medium heat. Add vermouth and simmer 1 minute. Add chicken broth and tomato juice; bring to a boil. Season with salt and pepper to taste and reduce heat. Simmer 10 to 12 minutes, or until sauce reduces by one half. Add diced lobster meat and heat through. Serve hot over red snapper.

### Beer Batter Fish

*4 servings*

1 pound fish fillets (flounder, grouper, or bass suggested)

1 1/2 cups homemade batter mix, recipe follows

1/3 cup lemon juice

2/3 cup beer

1 cup vegetable oil

Wash fish and pat dry on paper towels. Coat fish with 1/2 cup dry batter mix. In large bowl, combine remaining 1 cup of dry batter mix with lemon juice and beer; mixture will be foamy. Stir until it is the consistency of pancake batter. In a large skillet, heat oil over medium to medium high heat. Dip coated fish into the beer batter. Fry about 3 minutes or until golden brown on each side. Drain on paper towels. Keep warm in a 250° F oven until ready to serve. Serve with fresh lemon wedges and malt or balsamic vinegar, if desired.

Batter Mix:

1 1/2 cups flour

2 1/4 teaspoons baking powder

3/4 teaspoon baking soda

1 1/2 teaspoon salt

Combine all ingredients.

## Low Country Crab Cakes

*4 servings*

1 pound lump crab meat, picked

1 tablespoon capers

2 tablespoons green onions, chopped fine (use white and light green parts only)

1 tablespoon dry white wine

Cayenne pepper to taste

2 egg whites, beaten lightly

3 tablespoons flour

2 tablespoons olive oil

In a medium bowl, gently mix crab meat, capers, green onions and wine. Add Cayenne pepper to taste. Gently add egg whites and flour. Add more flour if necessary, but only enough to make the mixture stick together. Form into four cakes. Sauté in hot oil 3 to 4 minutes on each side, or until golden brown. Serve with lemon wedges or fresh tartar sauce.

## Fabulous Fish Chowder

*2 to 4 servings*

*1 cup onion, chopped*

*1/2 cup salt pork, diced finely (bacon may be substituted)*

*1 cup butter*

*1 cup raw potatoes, diced*

*1/2 cup water*

*2 tablespoons flour*

*2 cups milk*

*1 cup whipping cream*

*2 cups cooked fish, flaked*

*hot pepper sauce, to taste*

*In a saucepan, sautè onion and salt pork in butter. Cook over medium heat until tender, but not brown. Add potatoes and water. Cook until potatoes are tender. Stir in flour, cook 2 minutes. Stir in milk and cook 5 minutes, stirring constantly. Add cream and fish, heat through. Add hot pepper sauce to taste.*

## BAKED SHRIMP
*4 to 6 servings*

2 pounds large shrimp, peeled and deveined

1/4 cup sherry or dry white wine

1/2 cup butter, melted

1/4 cup fresh lemon juice

1/4 cup green onions, chopped

1/4 cup fresh parsley, chopped

1/4 teaspoon salt

1/4 cup Italian style bread crumbs

1/4 cup toasted almonds or pecans, chopped

Preheat oven to 400° F. Arrange shrimp in a single layer on baking sheet with shallow sides. Mix together sherry, butter and lemon juice. Pour evenly over shrimp. Sprinkle onions, parsley, salt, bread crumbs and nuts over shrimp.

Bake uncovered 20 minutes. Drizzle juice over shrimp and serve with crusty French bread. Can be prepared ahead, refrigerated and cooked just before serving.

## Pasta with Shrimp, Lemon and Tomatoes

*4 servings*

8 ounces pasta, (linguine, spaghetti or
    fettucini)

3 tablespoons olive oil

3 tablespoons butter

4 cloves garlic, minced

1 pound medium shrimp, uncooked

1/2 cup clam juice

1/3 cup oil packed sundried tomatoes, diced

1/4 cup fresh parsley, minced

zest of 1 lemon, removed in strips without
    white pith, cut julienne

salt and fresh ground pepper

Cook pasta according to package directions.
Toss with 1 tablespoon olive oil. Melt butter and
remaining oil. Sauté garlic until tender over
medium heat. Increase heat and sauté shrimp
until pink, about 2 minutes. Add clam juice
and pasta to pan. Cook over medium high
3 minutes. Add tomatoes, parsley and lemon
zest; season with salt and pepper.

Serve immediately.

## SHREDDED BEEF BURRITOS

*8 to 10 servings*

3 pounds boneless beef chuck roast

4 teaspoons chili powder

1 tablespoon olive oil

1 large onion, chopped fine

2 garlic cloves, minced

1 4-ounce can green chilies, chopped

1 teaspoon ground cumin

1 teaspoon dry oregano

1 8-ounce can tomato sauce

salt to taste

18 flour tortillas

2 medium avocados

1 tablespoon lime juice

to garnish: salsa, lettuce, Monterey Jack
cheese, shredded

Preheat oven to 350° F. Sprinkle all sides of beef with 3 teaspoons of chili powder. Heat oil in a nonstick frying pan over medium high heat. Add beef and brown well on both sides. Meanwhile, in 4-quart slow cooker, combine onion, garlic, and chilies. Place beef on top of onion mixture, and sprinkle with cumin, oregano, and remaining chili powder. Add tomato sauce. Cover and cook at low setting until beef is so tender it falls into shreds when prodded with a fork, about 9 to 10 hours. Preheat oven to 350° F. Remove beef from cooker and shred. Skim remaining liquid. Return shredded beef to cooker and season with salt. Cover and cook on high heat 15 to 20 minutes. While beef is cooking, stack tortillas and wrap in foil; bake 10 to 15 minutes or until heated through. Slice avocados and mix gently with lime juice. To make burritos, spoon shredded beef and avocado slices into a warm tortilla; garnish with salsa, lettuce and cheese. Fold in one end of tortilla; gently roll up tortilla to enclose filling.

191

### BLACK BEAN AND CHEESE TORTILLA PIE

*6 to 8 servings*

1 15-ounce package refrigerated pie crust

Filling:

3 tablespoons oil

1 cup onion, chopped

1/2 cup bell pepper, chopped

1 15-ounce can black beans, drained and rinsed

1/2 cup salsa

1 tablespoon fresh jalapeno pepper, minced (optional)

1/2 teaspoon chili powder (optional)

1/2 teaspoon Cayenne pepper (optional)

8 ounces Cheddar cheese, shredded

3 8-inch flour tortillas

Topping:

1/2 cup sour cream (optional)

Preheat oven to 350° F. Prepare pie crust according to package directions for a two-crust pie using a 9 or 10-inch deep dish pie pan. Heat oil in large skillet over medium-high heat. Add onion and bell pepper; stir until tender, about 5 minutes. Add beans, salsa, jalapeno peppers, chili powder and Cayenne pepper; simmer 7 to 10 minutes, stirring occasionally.

Spoon about 1/2 cup bean mixture into crust-lined pan. Sprinkle with 1/2 cup of cheese; top with tortilla. Repeat layering twice; sprinkle with remaining cheese. Top with second pie crust; seal and flute the edges. Cut slits in top crust.

Bake 40 to 50 minutes or until golden brown. Let stand 10 minutes before serving. Serve with sour cream.

SEAFOOD
DINNER MENU
FLORIDA STYLE

*Seafood and Florida go together like sun and fun. The best seafood meals begin with a great entree and this one's got it! It pairs the breezy flavors of Red Snapper and Lobster Sauce for the taste of Florida you're sure to love. Try this with Spinach Salad and the other recipes listed when you want to serve something out of the ordinary.*

*Frogmore*
**Pickled Shrimp**
*page 38*

**Cheddar Bread**
*page 70*

*Fresh Spinach Salad*
*page 97*

**Pasta Sauce**
**Florida Style**
*page 167*

**Tangy Asparagus**
*page 143*

**Red Snapper in**
**Lobster Sauce**
*page 185*

**Margarita Pie**
*page 214*

HOLBROOK
TRAVEL, INC.

### MARINADE FOR PORTOBELLA GRILLED MUSHROOMS

*4 servings*

1/2 cup olive oil

5 tablespoons red wine vinegar

5 cloves garlic, chopped fine

1/2 teaspoon oregano

1/2 teaspoon rosemary

1 teaspoon basil

1 tablespoon red onion, chopped fine

1 tablespoon brown sugar

salt and pepper to taste

4 Portobella mushrooms

fresh Parmesan cheese, grated coarse or into
   curls using a cheese slicer

4 hamburger buns

Combine marinade ingredients in a shallow dish. Brush and clean the Portobella mushrooms. Trim the woody tip of the stem ends. Place the mushrooms in the marinade. Marinate in the refrigerator 1 to 1 1/2 hours. Grill the mushrooms for 10 minutes per side and serve on toasted hamburger buns with Parmesan cheese curls.

## PLUM TOMATO CHUTNEY
*Makes about 3 cups*

8 garlic cloves, chopped

1/2 cup crystallized ginger, chopped fine

1 1/2 cups red wine vinegar, divided

1 35-ounce can plum tomatoes, undrained

1 1/2 cups sugar

2 teaspoons salt

1/2 teaspoon red pepper flakes

1/2 cup pine nuts

1/2 cup golden raisins

Combine garlic, ginger and 1/2 cup vinegar in food processor or blender and purée until smooth. Transfer to large saucepan. Add tomatoes with liquid, remaining 1 cup vinegar, sugar, salt and red pepper flakes. Place over medium-high heat and bring to a boil. Reduce heat to low and simmer until mixture coats spoon, about two hours.

Blend in pine nuts and raisins and simmer for 5 minutes. Let cool. Transfer to jars with tight-fitting lids. Refrigerate until ready to serve.

195

### CATALINA VENISON

*4 to 6 servings*

2 pounds fresh venison (backstrap loin
   recommended), cut into 1/4-inch
   thick steaks

1 8-ounce bottle Catalina-style dressing

flour for dredging

salt and pepper to taste

dash garlic powder

2 eggs

1/2 cup milk

2 tablespoons vegetable oil

In glass dish, pour Catalina dressing over
venison. Dressing should coat meat thoroughly.
Cover and marinate in the refrigerator 24 hours.

In medium bowl combine flour, salt, pepper
and garlic powder. In another medium bowl
lightly beat eggs and milk. Dip venison in egg
mixture and then dredge in flour mixture. Heat
vegetable oil in skillet and brown venison over
medium-low heat until tender.

Season to taste.

*Note:*
*May substitute bread crumbs for flour.*

*Desserts*

## Wilhelmina Johnson Center

Charmingly nestled in the northwest section of Gainesville is a special place called the Wilhelmina Johnson Center. Built in 1927 as the Alachua County Health Department, it served as a fire station from the 1940s until the late 1970s when it became an active community center.

The Center was named for Wilhelmina Johnson, a teacher from the surrounding neighborhood, whose tireless efforts helped revitalize the nearby community. Through her leadership, the neighborhood was able to receive block grant funds for the paving of streets, sidewalks, street lights and much, much more.

Today the Center continues to serve its neighborhood as a place for children and adults to participate in a variety of activities and organizations. The progression from Health Department to community center illustrates how a historic building can become the focal point for a better community in which to live.

THE PRECEDING PAGE PRESENTED BY THE VILLAGE RETIREMENT CENTER

# DESSERTS

### CAFÉ MOUSSE
*16 servings*

4 eggs, separated

3/4 cup sugar, divided

1 cup coffee flavored liqueur

2 8-ounce cartons non-dairy
  whipped topping

2 chocolate bars with almonds,
  chopped coarse

Beat egg yolks with 1/4 cup of sugar. Add 1 cup coffee flavored liqueur. Mix whipped topping into liqueur and sugar mixture.

Beat egg whites until they form peaks. Add 1/2 cup sugar. Fold into liqueur mixture. Freeze in individual glass serving dishes at least 3 hours. Top with chopped chocolate bars.

### FRESH MANGO SORBET
*6 servings*

2 large ripe mangoes, pitted and chopped

1 cup canned mango nectar

1/2 cup fresh lime juice

3/4 cup sugar

zest of one small lime

In a food processor, combine all of the ingredients and purée. Transfer the mixture to a medium-size bowl, cover with plastic wrap and refrigerate until very cold. Place mixture in an ice cream machine and freeze according to manufacturer's directions.

## Chocolate Chess Pie

*8 servings*

1 1/2 cups sugar

3 tablespoons cocoa

1/4 cup butter or margarine, softened

2 eggs, slightly beaten

1/4 teaspoon salt

1 5-ounce can evaporated milk

1 teaspoon vanilla extract

3/4 cup pecans, chopped

1 9-inch pie shell, unbaked

whipped cream, optional

Preheat oven to 350° F. Cream together sugar, cocoa and butter. Add eggs and beat with electric mixer 2 to 3 minutes. Stir in salt, milk and vanilla and mix well. Fold in pecans. Pour into pie shell and bake 35 to 45 minutes. Cool on wire rack, then refrigerate until serving. Serve with a dollop of whipped cream, if desired.

201

## COCONUT CREAM CHEESECAKE

*12 Servings*

Crust:

2/3 cup all-purpose flour

1 tablespoon sugar

5 tablespoons butter, well-chilled and cut into small pieces

Combine flour and sugar in large bowl. Using pastry blender or two knives, cut butter into the dry ingredients until mixture resembles coarse meal. Gather into a ball. Wrap in plastic wrap. Refrigerate 15 minutes.

Preheat oven to 325° F. Press dough into bottom of 10-inch springform pan. Bake until golden brown, 15 to 20 minutes. Cool slightly. Reduce oven temperature to 300° F.

Filling:

3 8-ounce packages cream cheese,
   room temperature

1 1/2 cups sugar

4 eggs, room temperature

2 egg yolks, room temperature

2 cups flaked coconut

1 cup whipping cream

1 teaspoon lemon juice

1 teaspoon vanilla extract

1 teaspoon almond extract

toasted coconut, optional for garnish

Using electric mixer, beat cream cheese and
sugar until smooth. Beat in eggs and yolks,
one at a time. Mix in flaked coconut,
whipping cream, lemon juice, vanilla extract
and almond extract.

Pour filling into crust. Bake at 300° F,
until edges of filling are firm, about
70 minutes. Let cheesecake cool completely.

Remove springform pan. Cover cheesecake
with plastic wrap. Refrigerate 4 hours. Just
before serving, sprinkle with toasted coconut.

203

### LEMON CHESS PIE
*Makes two 8 or 9-inch pies*

2 cups sugar

1 tablespoon cornmeal

1 tablespoon flour

4 eggs, unbeaten

1/4 cup butter, melted

1/4 cup milk

4 tablespoons fresh lemon juice

4 tablespoons of lemon zest

2 8 or 9-inch pie shells, unbaked

Preheat oven to 375° F. In a large bowl, combine sugar, cornmeal and flour; toss lightly with a fork. Add eggs, butter, milk, lemon juice and lemon zest. Beat until smooth and well blended. Pour mixture into uncooked pie shells. Bake 30 to 45 minutes until crusts are golden brown.

 *Idea!*

*Use a lemon zester, vegetable peeler or grater to remove only the yellow outer rind leaving the white pith.*

## HERITAGE CLUB
## MACADAMIA NUT PIE

*8 servings*

10 whole eggs

2 1/2 cups sugar

10 ounces butter

1 teaspoon salt

10 ounces Irish cream liqueur

2 cups corn syrup

5 ounces semi-sweet chocolate, diced

2 cups macadamia nuts, chopped

1 9-inch pie shell, unbaked

Preheat oven to 325° F. Mix together eggs, sugar, butter, salt, liqueur and corn syrup. Sprinkle chocolate over bottom of pie shell; top with nuts. Add egg mixture and bake for approximately 25 minutes. Cool overnight in refrigerator.

205

## MINI AMARETTO CHEESE CAKES

*Makes 6 dozen*

3 8-ounce packages cream cheese, softened

3 eggs

1 1/2 cups sugar

1 teaspoon vanilla extract

1 teaspoon almond extract

Preheat oven to 350° F. Mix all ingredients until smooth. Spoon mixture into paper lined mini muffin pans, filling about 3/4 full. Do not overfill. Bake 20 minutes. Cool in pans.

Topping:

1 cup sour cream

1/2 cup sugar

1 teaspoon vanilla extract

Combine all ingredients in a small bowl, mixing well. Spread on top of cooled cheesecakes. Refrigerate mini-cakes until ready to serve.

## Amazon Bars

*Makes 24 bars*

1/2 cup butter

2 dozen whole graham crackers, crushed

1 14-ounce can sweetened condensed milk

1 7-ounce package coconut flakes

1 6-ounce package semi-sweet
  chocolate chips

1 cup Brazil nuts, chopped

1/2 cup cashews, chopped

Preheat oven to 350° F. Melt butter in 9 x 13-inch pan. Sprinkle graham cracker crumbs over butter; press together to form crust. Pour sweetened condensed milk over crust and spread with spatula. Sprinkle on coconut and semi-sweet chocolate chips; cover with nuts. Bake 30 minutes. Let cool in pan before cutting. Serve at room temperature or slightly chilled.

## LIME MERINGUE PIE

*8 to 10 servings*

Crust:

1 1/3 cups graham crackers,
crushed fine

1 tablespoon pecans, ground fine

1/4 cup sugar

1 1/2 tablespoons flour

5 tablespoons butter, chilled and cut
into small pieces

Preheat oven to 350° F. In a food processor, combine graham crackers, pecans, sugar and flour. Process 15 seconds. Add the butter and process until crumbs begin to cling together. Press into 9 or 10-inch pie plate. Bake 8 minutes. Cool completely on wire rack.

Filling:

4 eggs, separated (reserve whites for
meringue. Place in a stainless steel bowl.)

1 14-ounce can sweetened condensed milk

2/3 cup lime juice, freshly squeezed
(Key lime, if available)

Lower temperature of oven to 325° F. Using an electric mixer, beat egg yolks on high speed until thick and light yellow in color. Turn off mixer; add condensed milk. Mix on slow speed. Add half the lime juice and mix. Pour in the remaining juice. Mix until blended. Pour into the cooled pie crust. Bake 8 to 10 minutes. Cool on wire rack.

Meringue:

4 egg whites

3/4 cup granulated sugar

In a stainless steel bowl, combine sugar and egg whites. Place bowl in a pan of warm water and stir until sugar is dissolved. Remove bowl from pan of water and, with very clean beaters, beat egg whites until stiff peaks form. Spread meringue over top of pie. Broil until golden brown. Watch carefully so that the meringue will not burn.

 *Idea!*

*Make sure to spread beyond edges of pie plate, because meringue shrinks as it cools.*

## RASPBERRY VELVET TART

*8 servings*

Crust:

3/4 cup cake flour

3/4 cup all-purpose flour

1/4 cup sugar

1/2 cup unsalted butter, chilled and cut
   into pieces

1 egg yolk

1 tablespoon whipping cream

2 tablespoons cold water

Mix flours and sugar in large bowl. Cut butter into flour until mixture resembles coarse meal. Beat egg yolk with cream to blend; pour over flour mixture and stir until dough comes together. Add water to bind dough, if necessary. Gather dough into ball and flatten into a disk. Wrap in plastic and refrigerate 30 minutes. (Dough may be prepared a day ahead. Let dough soften before continuing.)

Roll dough out on lightly floured surface to 1/8 inch thick. Roll up dough on rolling pin and transfer to 9-inch tart pan with removable bottom. Trim and finish edges. Refrigerate crust 30 minutes.

Preheat oven to 350° F. Line pastry with foil or parchment and fill with dried beans or pie weights. Bake 15 minutes. Remove beans and foil and continue baking crust until golden brown, about 15 minutes. Cool crust completely on wire rack.

Filling:

12 ounces white chocolate, chopped

1/2 cup whipping cream, hot

1/4 cup unsalted butter,
   room temperature

2 cups fresh raspberries

Melt white chocolate in top of double boiler over simmering water, stirring until smooth. Add cream and butter; mix well. Remove from heat. Distribute raspberries evenly over bottom of prepared crust, reserving a few for garnish. Pour chocolate mixture over berries, filling crust completely. Refrigerate until firm, about 1 hour (can be prepared 1 day ahead). Garnish with white chocolate leaves, if desired (recipe follows). Cover and refrigerate. Let stand at room temperature 1 hour before serving.

White Chocolate Leaves:

3 ounces white chocolate, chopped

16 small leaves with 1/8-inch stems,
   freshly picked leaves such as rose,
   gardenia, lemon, camilla or plastic ones
   may be used.

Melt white chocolate in top of double boiler over simmering water, stirring until smooth. Spread in thin layer over veined underside of leaves being careful not to drip over edges. Refrigerate until firm, about 30 minutes. Gently peel off leaves, starting at stem end. (Can be prepared one week ahead. Cover in airtight container and refrigerate.)

211

# DESSERTS

## RASPBERRY CLAFOUTI
### (OVEN-BAKED PUFF PANCAKE)
*8 servings*

3 eggs

1 1/4 cups milk

2/3 cup all-purpose flour

1/3 cup sugar

1 teaspoon vanilla

1 teaspoon sherry

1/4 teaspoon nutmeg

1/8 teaspoon salt

1 1/2 cups fresh raspberries

whipped cream

Preheat oven to 350° F. In a small mixing bowl, beat eggs with electric mixer until foamy. Add milk, flour, sugar, vanilla, sherry, nutmeg and salt; beat with electric mixer on low speed until smooth. Pour batter into greased 9-inch quiche dish or pie plate. If desired, reserve a few raspberries for garnish. Sprinkle remaining raspberries over batter.

Bake 40 to 45 minutes or until knife inserted in center comes out clean. Let stand 15 minutes. Garnish with whipped cream and reserved raspberries.

 *Idea!*

*Bake the dessert during dinner, then serve it warm from the oven.*

## RED VELVET CAKE

*8 to 10 servings*

2 cups sugar

1 cup vegetable oil

2 large eggs

1 teaspoon vinegar

1 ounce red food coloring

2 tablespoons cocoa

2 1/2 cups flour

1 cup sour cream

1 teaspoon baking soda

1 teaspoon salt

1 teaspoon vanilla extract

Preheat oven to 350° F. Grease and flour three 8 or 9-inch round cake pans. Cream together sugar and oil. Add eggs. Combine vinegar, food coloring and cocoa in separate bowl. Add to sugar mixture. Blend. Alternate adding flour and sour cream to mixture. Add soda, salt and vanilla. Pour into prepared pans and bake 25 to 30 minutes. Cool.

Icing:

1 1-pound box powdered sugar

1 8-ounce package cream cheese

1/2 cup butter or margarine, softened

1 teaspoon vanilla extract

1 cup pecans, chopped

Cream together sugar, cream cheese and butter. Add vanilla and beat well. Stir in pecans. Ice the top, sides and between layers of cooled cake.

213

### MARGARITA PIE
*8 servings*

1 1/4 cups pretzels, crushed fine

10 tablespoons butter, melted

1/2 cup sugar

1 14-ounce can condensed milk

1/3 cup fresh lime juice

2 to 4 tablespoons tequila

2 tablespoons triple sec

8 ounces whipped topping

Combine pretzel crumbs, butter and sugar. Press firmly on bottom and sides of slightly buttered 9-inch pie plate. Combine condensed milk, lime juice, tequila and triple sec. Fold in half of the whipped topping. Pour into prepared crust. Spread remaining whipped topping over pie. Freeze or chill until firm.

## APPLE PIE WITH FRENCH PIE PASTRY

*8 servings*

1/2 cup butter
1/2 cup orange juice
1 cup sugar
4 to 6 cups apples, peeled and cored
dash cinnamon
1/2 recipe French Pie Crust (see below)

Preheat oven to 375° F. Combine butter, orange juice and sugar in heavy pot and boil until it becomes a light syrup. Peel and core apples and cut them into wedges. Add to syrup and cook until apples are transparent. Add cinnamon. Drain off most of the syrup and reserve. Pour apples into unbaked pie crust. Bake 30 to 35 minutes. Reheat syrup and serve with slices of pie.

French Pie Pastry:
2 cups flour, sifted
1/2 teaspoon salt
1/4 teaspoon sugar
1/2 cup butter, chilled and cut into pieces
3 tablespoons vegetable shortening, chilled
5 tablespoons water, chilled

Combine flour, salt and sugar. Cut in butter and shortening with pastry cutter or fork until mixture is coarse like oatmeal. Add water and quickly blend with hands. Press into a ball. Press out with palm of hand. Gather and divide, forming two balls. Sprinkle lightly with flour. Cover with plastic wrap. Refrigerate or freeze until needed. Roll out one ball to make crust for Apple Pie above.

215

### FRESH FRUIT COBBLER

*8 servings*

1/2 cup butter

1 cup milk

1 cup self-rising flour

1 cup sugar

4 cups fresh fruit (peaches, apples, blueberries, etc.), sweetened to taste

Preheat oven to 375° F. Melt butter and put in deep dish pie pan. Stir in milk, flour and sugar. Pour the fruit over the mixture. Do not mix! Bake 40 minutes. The bottom will rise to the top to form the crust.

 ***Idea!***

*To make self-rising flour, add 2 teaspoons of baking powder to regular flour.*

### SWEET POTATO PIE

*16 servings*

1 cup sugar

1/2 cup butter, melted

3 eggs

2 cups sweet potatoes, cooked, peeled and mashed slightly (about 4 medium)

1 tablespoon vanilla extract

2 9-inch pie shells, unbaked

Preheat oven to 350° F. Using an electric mixer, combine sugar and butter; mix well. Add eggs one at a time and beat. Stir in potatoes and vanilla; mix well. Pour into pie shells. Bake for 1 hour or until knife comes out clean.

 ***Idea!***

*You may use pumpkin instead of sweet potatoes.*

# ENGLISH TOFFEE SQUARES

*6 Servings*

1 cup vanilla wafer crumbs
  (about 18 wafers crushed)

1 cup pecans, chopped

1 cup powdered sugar

1/4 pound butter

3 egg yolks, beaten

1 1/2 ounces bittersweet chocolate,
  melted and cooled

1/2 teaspoon vanilla

3 egg whites, at room temperature,
  beaten into stiff peaks

whipped cream for topping (optional)

Mix together crumbs and pecans. Spread half of this wafer mixture evenly over the bottom of a buttered 9 x 9-inch pan. Cream together sugar and butter until well mixed. Add the beaten egg yolks, melted chocolate and vanilla. Carefully fold in egg whites. Spread evenly over the wafer mixture. Sprinkle reserved wafer mixture over the top. Cover tightly with plastic wrap and refrigerate overnight. Cut into squares and serve with lightly sweetened whipped cream, if desired.

## APPLE CAKE
*12 servings*

12 apples, peeled and diced

1 1/4 cups oil

2 cups sugar

3 eggs, beaten

3 cups flour

1 teaspoon baking soda

1 teaspoon salt

1/8 teaspoon nutmeg or cinnamon

yogurt or ice cream, optional

Mix apples, oil, sugar, eggs, flour, baking soda, salt and nutmeg or cinnamon until blended. Pour into a well greased 9 x 13-inch pan. Place pan in cold oven, heat oven to 325° F and cook 35 to 45 minutes. Top with yogurt or ice cream, if desired.

## PEACH PERFECT

*4 servings*

10 tablespoons butter

1/2 cup brown sugar

1/4 teaspoon cinnamon

2 tablespoons coconut

5 fresh peaches, peeled, pitted and cut into wedges

2 teaspoons peach liqueur, may substitute 1 teaspoon vanilla extract

4 tablespoons 151 proof rum (no substitutions)

vanilla ice cream

In a medium skillet, melt butter over medium heat. Add brown sugar, cinnamon, coconut and heat, stirring constantly until sugar is dissolved. Stir in fresh peaches. Heat 2 minutes, add peach liqueur and stir to coat peaches. Heat one additional minute, remove pan from heat and add rum and ignite mixture (use caution—flames will rise 1-2 feet over pan). After flame has extinguished itself, serve mixture over ice cream.

219

### CHOCOLATE CARAMEL SQUARES

*Makes 24 squares*

1 18 1/4-ounce package chocolate
  cake mix

2/3 cup evaporated milk, divided

3/4 cup butter, melted

1 14-ounce package caramels,
  wrappers removed

1 cup semi-sweet chocolate chips

1/4 cup semi-sweet chocolate chips,
  optional frosting

Preheat oven to 350° F. Blend dry cake mix with 1/3 cup evaporated milk and butter. Pour half of this mixture into a well greased 9 x 13-inch pan. Bake for 6 to 10 minutes. Melt caramels with the remaining 1/3 cup evaporated milk over low heat. Remove cake mixture from oven. Sprinkle cake mixture with the semi-sweet chips and pour melted caramels over all. Carefully spread remaining batter over top. Smooth batter with spoon not mixing with caramel mixture. Bake 15 to 18 minutes or longer. Remove from oven.

After removing from oven, sprinkle more semi-sweet chips over top for optional frosting and let sit for 5 minutes, then spread.

## Delectable Chocolate Pie

*8 servings*

Cornflake Crust:

1 cup cornflake crumbs

1/4 cup butter, softened

2 tablespoons sugar

Mix cornflake crumbs, butter and sugar. Pat into a 9-inch pie pan.

Filling:

1 1/2 cups semi-sweet chocolate chips

dash of salt

3 eggs

1 teaspoon vanilla

1 cup heavy cream

whipped cream, for topping

shaved chocolate, optional

Melt semi-sweet chocolate chips in double broiler over hot but not boiling water; set aside. Remove from heat and quickly stir in dash of salt and one egg, mixing well. Separate 2 eggs and add egg yolks to mixture, one at a time, beating well after each addition. Stir in vanilla. Beat 2 egg whites stiff, but not dry. Whip heavy cream then fold cream and egg whites into chocolate mixture. Pour into crust and chill. Top with whipped cream and shaved chocolate.

ALL CHOCOLATE DESSERTS

*If you're craving chocolate, then this menu's for you! It only takes one bite of our delicious Chocolate Pecan Pie and you'll fall in love with it. Try this luscious menu for an out of the ordinary dessert buffet. But beware, guests will think it's so good, you may miss having some yourself!*

*Chocolate Pecan Pie page 229*

*Heritage Club Macadamia Nut Pie page 205*

*Delectable Chocolate Pie page 221*

*Cafe Mousse page 200*

*Chocolate Chess Pie page 201*

221

THE JUNIOR LEAGUE OF GAINESVILLE 1996-1997 PROVISIONAL CLASS

## ORANGE COOKIES

*makes 60 cookies*

zest of 1/2 fresh orange, grated
juice of 1/2 fresh orange
1/2 cup shortening
1 cup sugar
1 egg
1/2 cup sour milk or buttermilk
3 cups flour
1 teaspoon baking powder
1/2 teaspoon baking soda

222

Preheat oven to 350° F. Grate orange rind then squeeze the orange for juice. Save this mixture. Cream together shortening and sugar. Add egg, orange juice, orange zest, sour milk and mix well. Add flour, baking powder and soda, mixing well. Drop by teaspoon onto a greased cookie sheet. Bake 15 minutes. Remove to cool on wire rack.

Frosting:

1 16-ounce package powdered sugar
juice of 1/2 fresh orange
2 tablespoons butter, softened
zest of 1/2 fresh orange

Combine powdered sugar and orange juice. Stir in butter and orange zest. Beat until smooth. Frost cookies when cool.

 ***Idea!***

*To make sour milk, combine 1/2 cup milk and 2 1/4 teaspoons lemon juice (it will curdle)*

## COCONUT PIE

*8 servings*

3 eggs, separated

3 tablespoons flour or
   1/3 cup cornstarch

2/3 cup sugar

1/4 teaspoon salt

2 cups milk

2 tablespoons butter or margarine

1 teaspoon vanilla

1 cup coconut, shredded

1/8 teaspoon cream of tartar

6 tablespoons sugar

1 8- or 9-inch pie shell, uncooked

Preheat oven to 400° F. Beat egg yolks. Mix flour and sugar together and combine gradually with egg yolks, adding milk a little at a time, whisking until smooth. Cook over medium heat until mixture thickens. Remove, add butter, vanilla and coconut. Mix together and pour into pie shell. Beat the egg whites and creme of tartar with six tablespoons sugar (2 tablespoons at a time) until stiff and holds its shape. Spread over pie and brown for 10 minutes.

## LEMON FLUFF PIE

*8 servings*

1 3-ounce package lemon flavored gelatin

1 1/2 tablespoons sugar

1 cup boiling water

1/4 cup plus 2 tablespoons cold water

2 tablespoons fresh lemon juice

Combine gelatin, sugar, and boiling water, stirring 2 minutes until gelatin dissolves. Stir in cold water and lemon juice. Chill 30 minutes or until mixture is the consistency of unbeaten egg whites.

1 8-ounce carton lemon yogurt

1 8-ounce frozen whipped topping, thawed

2 teaspoons grated lemon rind

1 9-inch graham cracker crust

Garnishes:
Lemon slices, lemon zest, fresh mint sprigs

Fold yogurt, whipped topping, and lemon rind into gelatin mixture; spoon into crust. Chill in refrigerator at least 3 hours. Garnish, if desired.

## CRUMB CAKE

*8 to 10 servings*

1 16-ounce box graham crackers, crumbled

2 cups sugar

1 cup butter

5 eggs, room temperature

1 20-ounce can crushed pineapple, drained

1 14-ounce package flaked coconut

1 cup nuts, chopped

1 cup milk, room temperature

1 teaspoon lemon extract

1/2 teaspoon salt

2 teaspoons baking powder

Preheat oven to 350° F. Butter a bundt pan. In a very large mixing bowl, cream together sugar and butter, add eggs one at a time, beating them thoroughly. Add remaining ingredients. Pour into pan. Bake 1 hour and 15 minutes. Cool in pan.

Serve with whipped cream or ice cream if desired.

### DEEP CHOCOLATE CAKE
#### WITH COCONUT BROILED TOPPING
*10 to 12 servings*

Cake:

1/4 cup cocoa and 1/2 cup very hot water

1/2 cup and 1/3 cup flour

1/4 teaspoon baker powder

1/2 teaspoon baking soda

3/4 cup sugar

1/4 teaspoon salt

1/4 cup shortening

1 egg

Topping:

1/2 stick margarine or butter

1/2 cup dark brown sugar

1/2 teaspoon vanilla

3/4 cup coconut

1/2 cup chopped pecans

2 tablespoons milk

Preheat oven to 350° F. Combine cocoa and very hot water and mix until smooth. Let cool. In a separate bowl, mix together all the flour, baking powder, baking soda, sugar and salt. Add shortening and cooled cocoa mixture. Mix with electric mixer on a medium low speed for 2 minutes. Add egg and continue beating for 2 more minutes. Bake 15 to 20 minutes in a greased 8-inch square baking dish. After cake comes out of oven, prepare topping. In a saucepan melt butter; add brown sugar, vanilla, coconut and pecans. Melt over low heat and stir until cara-melized; add milk (keep on low heat). Spread like frosting on cake. Place entire cake with topping under preheated broiler. Keep an eye on cake until brown (toasted golden brown), approximately 1 minute. Do not burn.

## CHEESECAKE BARS
*8 to 10 servings*

1/3 cup butter

1/3 cup brown sugar

1 cup flour

1/2 cup chopped nuts

Preheat oven to 350° F. Cream together butter and sugar. Add flour, nuts, and blend into a crumbly mixture. Reserve 1 cup for topping. Press remaining mixture into an 8-inch square pan. Bake 12 to 15 minutes.

Filling:

1/4 cup sugar

1 8-ounce package cream cheese, softened

1 egg

2 tablespoons milk

1/2 teaspoon vanilla

Preheat oven to 350° F. Combine the sugar, cream cheese, egg, milk and vanilla until smooth and creamy. Spread mixture over baked crust. Sprinkle with reserved crumbs on top. Bake 25 minutes. Cut into bars when cooled. Refrigerate leftovers.

## PUMPKIN SQUARES

*12 to 16 servings*

1 3/4 cups flour, unsifted

1/3 cup brown sugar

1/3 cup sugar

1 cup chilled butter or margarine, cut into small pieces

1 cup chopped pecans

Preheat oven to 350° F. In medium bowl, combine flour and sugars. Cut in margarine until crumbled. Stir in nuts. Reserving 1 cup crumb mixture, press remainder firmly on bottom and halfway up sides of 7 x 12-inch baking dish.

228

1 16-ounce can pumpkin

1 14-ounce can condensed milk (may use light)

2 eggs

2 teaspoons ground cinnamon

1/2 teaspoon ground allspice

1/2 teaspoon salt

In a large mixing bowl, add pumpkin, milk, eggs, cinnamon, allspice and salt. Mix well and pour into baking dish. Top with the reserved crumb mixture. Bake 55 minutes or until golden brown. Cool. Cut into squares. Serve with ice cream or whipped cream. Refrigerate leftovers.

## CHOCOLATE PECAN PIE

*6 to 8 servings*

2 large eggs, beaten

1 cup sugar

1/2 cup unsalted butter, melted

1/4 cup bourbon

1/4 cup coffee flavored liqueur

1/4 cup cornstarch

1 cup chopped pecans

6 ounces semi-sweet chocolate morsels

1 9-inch pie shell, unbaked

Preheat oven to 350° F. In mixing bowl, combine eggs, sugar, butter, bourbon, coffee liqueur, cornstarch, pecans and chocolate morsels in this order. Pour into pie shell and bake 45 minutes. Serve pie warm or at room temperature.

## PEANUT BUTTER PIE

*8 servings*

4-ounce package cream cheese, softened

1 cup powdered sugar, sifted

1/3 cup peanut butter

1/3 cup milk, may use 1% or 2% milk

1 8-ounce frozen whipped topping, may use light

1 9-inch graham cracker crust

Blend cream cheese, powdered sugar and peanut butter. Add milk slowly; beat until smooth and fluffy. Fold in whipped topping. Pour into pie shell. Freeze 2 hours.

## PISTACHIO POUND CAKE
*10 to 12 servings*

Cake:

1 box yellow cake mix

2 3 3/8-ounce packages instant Pistachio pudding

1/2 cup vegetable oil

1/2 cup milk

1/2 cup water

5 eggs

Preheat oven to 350° F. Grease and flour a bundt pan. In mixing bowl, Combine cake mix, pudding mix, oil, milk, water and eggs. Mix together until smooth. Pour into bundt pan and bake for 1 hour. Cool. Sprinkle with powdered sugar or drizzle white icing.

White Icing:

1 box powdered sugar

1 teaspoon almond extract

1/8 cup milk

1/4 cup pistachios or almonds, chopped for garnish, optional

Combine the sugar, almond extract and milk together. Drizzle over cake after it has cooled. Garnish with nuts, if desired.

 ***Idea!***

*We received many versions of this versatile pound cake for recipe testing. Although it is not technically a "scratch" cake, it is easy, convenient and delicious. Substitute your favorite flavors and keep these ingredients on hand. You'll always be ready with a beautiful cake to take along or give.*

## PEANUT BUTTER CHOCOLATE SQUARES
*16 to 20 servings*

1 cup butter or margarine
1 cup peanut butter, creamy or crunchy
1 16-ounce box powdered sugar, sifted
1 1/2 cup graham cracker crumbs
1 12-ounce package chocolate chips, melted

Melt butter in saucepan. Remove from heat. Stir in peanut butter, powdered sugar and graham cracker crumbs. Mix well and press mixture into a 9 x 13-inch ungreased pan. Spread melted chocolate chips evenly over top. Chill at least 30 minutes and cut into squares. Keep refrigerated.

231

## POPPY SEED CAKE

3/4 cup poppy seeds

3/4 cup whole milk

2 cups flour

1/2 teaspoon salt

2 teaspoons baking powder

3/4 cup butter

1 1/2 cups sugar

4 egg whites, slightly beaten

1 teaspoon vanilla

Soak poppy seeds in milk 4 to 5 hours or overnight. Sift together flour, salt and baking powder. Set aside.

Cream together butter and sugar. Add poppy seed and milk mixture, alternating with flour mixture, to the butter and sugar. Fold in egg whites and vanilla. Pour into 3 greased and floured 8-inch round cake pans. Bake 30 minutes at 350° F.

Filling:

1 cup sugar

2 cups whole milk

3 tablespoons cornstarch

4 egg yolks, slightly beaten

1 cup nuts, chopped

In top of double boiler, combine sugar, milk and cornstarch. Cook over boiling water 10 minutes or until mixture thickens. Remove from heat. Pour half of the hot mixture into the beaten eggs, stirring constantly. When smooth, return eggs to the hot mixture and cook until thickened. Remove from heat, stir in nuts, then cool. When filling and the layers of cake have cooled, assemble the layers with the filling between each layer.

Icing:

1/2 cup butter

3 cups powdered sugar

4 tablespoons cocoa

2 tablespoons vanilla

3 tablespoons milk

Cream butter, sugar and cocoa. Add vanilla and milk. Mix well. Spread on top of cake and let drip off of the sides of the cake.

233

## ESPRESSO ICE CREAM PIE
### WITH CARAMEL & RASPBERRIES
*6 to 8 servings*

Pie:

1 quart vanilla ice cream

4 tablespoons instant espresso coffee

1 9-inch chocolate crumb pie shell, following instructions for crisping, frozen

1/2 pint fresh raspberries (or fresh strawberries) for garnish

To Prepare Pie:

In a food processor fitted with metal blade, process ice cream and instant coffee using the pulse switch. Spoon mixture into frozen crust. Freeze.

Caramel Sauce:

1 cup sugar

1 cup water

1 cup whipping cream

1/8 teaspoon salt

1 teaspoon vanilla extract

To Prepare Sauce:

In a large saucepan combine sugar and water. Cook over medium heat, without stirring, for 10 to 15 minutes or until sugar turns a light golden brown. Monitor closely towards end of cooking time. Remove from heat, add whipping cream and stir until smooth. If sauce becomes hard, return briefly to heat. Allow sauce to cool 30 minutes at room temperature. Stir in salt and vanilla. Transfer to blender and blend until very smooth. Chill.

Presentation: Ten minutes before serving, remove pie from freezer. Pour chilled sauce to cover the bottoms of 6 to 8 dessert plates. Slice pie. Place each slice on plate over the sauce. Garnish with fruit and serve immediately.

## Fresh Blueberry Pie

*8 servings*

2 pints fresh blueberries, divided

1 cup sugar, divided

1 cup water

3 tablespoons cornstarch

1/2 teaspoon salt

2 teaspoons fresh lemon juice

1 teaspoon vanilla

1 8- or 9-inch pie shell, unbaked

Boil 1 pint of blueberries with 1/2 cup sugar and water for 5 minutes. Mix remaining 1/2 cup sugar with cornstarch and salt. Stir hot blueberry mixture into sugar and cornstarch mixture to make a paste. Cool until thickened. Add lemon juice and vanilla.

Add remaining pint of blueberries to pie shell; pour cooled blueberry mixture into pie shell. Chill and served with whipped cream or ice cream.

235

# DESSERTS

NOTES:

...................................................

...................................................

...................................................

...................................................

...................................................

...................................................

...................................................

...................................................

...................................................

...................................................

...................................................

...................................................

...................................................

...................................................

Children's Choices

## The Cracker Farm
### at Morningside Nature Park

There's a special feeling you get when visiting the Florida Farm exhibit at Morningside Nature Center. As you walk along the trail to the Cracker Farm, a working turn-of-the-century farm, you almost step back in time to a place where life seems simpler.

You'll be surrounded by "heirlooms" from the past as you discover a reconstructed log farmhouse, originally built in 1840, and an 1880s barn with livestock. Children are especially delighted to see the farm animals. A windmill, family garden, old tools and furnishings add to the ambiance.

The Junior League of Gainesville provided funding to help support the development of Morningside Nature Center's Cracker Farm, which opened and was dedicated on July 4, 1976. Additional funding from our League also helped in such areas as restoration and a part-time public relations position. This project from our past continues to be beneficial to the children of our community.

THE PRECEDING PAGE PRESENTED BY THE PAST PRESIDENTS OF
THE JUNIOR LEAGUE OF GAINESVILLE AS LISTED ON PAGE 241.

# Children's Choices

### Jack's Green Bean Bundles

*6 servings*

1 pound fresh green beans, trimmed
    and left whole

water

10 strips of bacon, cut in half

1 cup butter

1/2 cup brown sugar

Preheat oven to 375°F. Add enough water to cover beans in a pot, bring to a boil. Reduce heat to medium; cook 10 minutes. Drain water from beans. Arrange beans into small bundles. Wrap one strip of bacon around each bundle and place in 9 x 13-inch baking dish. Melt butter and brown sugar. Pour over bean bundles. Bake 45 minutes to 1 hour.

240

### Cornflake Chicken Strips

*6 servings*

2 1/2 to 3 cups cornflakes

4 boneless, skinless chicken breasts,
    cut into strips

1/4 cup butter or margarine, melted

2 to 3 tablespoons sesame seeds

garlic salt

pepper

Preheat oven to 375°F. Crush cornflakes in resealable plastic bag. Dip chicken strips in butter and shake in plastic bag with cornflake mixture. Place coated chicken in baking pan, sprayed with non-stick coating. Season with sesame seeds, salt and pepper. Bake 30 minutes.

## More Macaroni and Cheese, If You Please

*8 to 10 servings*

4 tablespoons butter

4 tablespoons flour

2 1/2 cups milk

12 ounces sharp Cheddar cheese, shredded

1/2 teaspoon salt

dash of pepper

1 16-ounce package small elbow macaroni, cooked
   according to directions

Preheat oven to 375°F. Melt butter slowly so that it does
not brown. Blend in flour. Add milk gradually, stirring
constantly. When sauce thickens and begins to bubble
reduce heat. Add cheese, reserving 1/2 cup for topping,
salt and pepper. Combine macaroni and sauce. Spoon into
greased casserole and sprinkle with remaining cheese.
Bake for 30 minutes.

## Cheese Sandwich Olé

**(If your children are bored with
the same old grilled cheese
sandwich, try this!)**

*1 serving*

2 6 or 8-inch flour tortillas, (found in grocer's
   refrigerated section)

1 slice American or Cheddar cheese, or other favorite
   cheese, may use shredded cheese

Cover a tortilla with cheese slice or shredded cheese. Top
with another tortilla. In a non-stick skillet (or one
prepared with non-stick spray, butter or margarine) heat
sandwich on both sides until cheese is melted. Let cool
and cut into quarters for a neat triangle treat.

241

## Spaghetti and Meatballs

*8 to 10 servings*

2 pounds hamburger meat

1 cup bread crumbs

1 teaspoon Italian seasonings

2 eggs

4 cups prepared spaghetti sauce

1 16 ounce box of spaghetti

Preheat oven to 375°F. Combine hamburger, bread crumbs, Italian seasonings, and eggs together. Shape into 1-inch meatballs. Bake for 25 to 30 minutes until brown. Heat spaghetti sauce and place meatballs in sauce and simmer for 20 minutes. Cook spaghetti according to directions. To serve, put spaghetti on plate and put sauce and meatballs on top.

242

## Sweet Pineapple Surprise

*8 servings*

4 cups fresh bread crumbs, use
    4 hamburger buns

1 20-ounce can pineapple chunks, drained

3 eggs beaten

2 cups sugar

1 cup butter, melted

Preheat oven to 350°F. Toss bread crumbs and pineapple chunks together in a bowl and place in a greased 2-quart baking dish. Combine eggs, sugar and butter. Pour over pineapple and bread mixture. Bake 30 minutes.

Can be prepared and refrigerated overnight before baking. Reheats well. Great with ham.

## Tennessee Apple Salad

6 to 8 servings

1/2 cup mayonnaise

1 tablespoon sugar

1/2 teaspoon lemon juice

1 cup non-dairy whipped topping

3 cups apples, chopped
   (about 4 medium apples)

1/2 cup celery, chopped

1/2 cup seedless red grapes, halved

1/2 cup walnuts, chopped

cinnamon

Combine mayonnaise, sugar, lemon juice and whipped topping; set aside. Combine apples, celery, grapes and walnuts. Stir dressing into apple mixture. Mix well. Sprinkle with cinnamon. Chill.

## Cabana Banana Slaw
(Don't let your mom and dad eat it all!)
6 to 8 servings

1 16-ounce package slaw mix (shredded cabbage and
   carrots, in produce section)

3/4 cup mayonnaise

1 teaspoon white vinegar

1/2 teaspoon salt

3 large bananas, chopped or sliced

Combine slaw mix, mayonnaise, vinegar and salt. Fold in bananas. Chill and serve.

## Lasagna Roll-Ups

*6 to 8 servings*

8 lasagna noodles, cooked according to directions, drain and lay flat

1 tablespoon olive oil

2 garlic cloves, minced

1 10-ounce package frozen chopped spinach, thawed and well drained

1 cup fat free Ricotta cheese

1 teaspoon salt

1 1/2 cups Mozzarella cheese, shredded

1 28-ounce jar spaghetti sauce

1/2 cup fresh parsley, chopped

Heat oil in skillet over medium and sauté garlic 2 minutes or until tender. In a medium bowl, combine spinach, ricotta, salt, garlic and half the Mozzarella cheese. Spread each lasagna noodle with cup of spinach mixture. Roll up firmly, jelly-roll fashion. Pour spaghetti sauce into skillet and place lasagna rolls seam side down in skillet. Bring to a boil, then reduce heat to low, cover and simmer 10 minutes. Sprinkle with remaining Mozzarella, cover and simmer 3 to 5 minutes longer or until rolls are heated through. Garnish with a parsley.

## Cloud 9 Fruit Dip

1 cup powered sugar

12 ounces cream cheese

7 ounces marshmallow creme

8 ounces sour cream

2 teaspoons vanilla

2 teaspoons almond extract

2 teaspoons cinnamon

Mix all ingredients and refrigerate. Sprinkle with cinnamon.

## Pirate's Corn Delight

*10 to 12 servings*

1 cup butter or margarine, melted

1 8-ounce cream cheese, softened

4 11-ounce cans shoe peg corn, drained

1 4-ounce can green chilies, chopped

Preheat oven to 350°F. Whisk together butter and cream cheese until smooth. Add corn and green chilies, mix well. Spoon into baking dish; bake 30 minutes.

**Young Chefs' Checklist:**

1. Always check with an adult before you begin cooking.

2. Read the whole recipe before you start.

3. Put on an apron or old clothes.

4. Wash your hands.

5. Prepare your recipe.

6. Turn appliances off when you are finished.

Beverages

### Lazy Day Lemonade
*1 1/2 quarts*

3/4 cup fresh lemon juice (about 5 medium lemons)

1/2 cup sugar

2 cups of cold water

1 cup ice cubes

lemon slices

Combine lemon juice and sugar until sugar is dissolved.
Add water and ice. Stir well. Garnish with lemon slices.

### Flippin' Fruit Smoothies
*1 serving*

1 banana

6 strawberries

1 slice cantaloupe, rind removed and chopped

3 ice cubes

1/2 cup peach or pear nectar

Combine ingredients in blender until smooth. Pour in large
glass with silly straw. Kids will flip over these!

 idea!

Use miniature marshmallows to hold
candles on a decorated cake.

## Delicious Apple Crisp

*6 servings*

6 or 7 apples

1 cup flour

1 1/2 cups sugar

1/2 teaspoon salt

1 teaspoon baking powder

1 unbeaten egg

1/3 cup butter

Preheat oven to 350°F. Prepare and slice apples. Place apples in a 2-quart baking dish. Combine flour, sugar, salt and baking powder in bowl. Add egg and mix with fork until crumbly. Spread over apples. Dot with butter or melt butter and pour over top. Bake 30 minutes.

## Peanut Butter Kisses

*makes 18 cookies*

1 cup smooth peanut butter

1 egg

1 cup sugar

chocolate kisses

Preheat oven to 350°F. Combine peanut butter, egg and sugar; mix well and roll into small balls. Place on ungreased cookie sheet. Bake 10 to 15 minutes. Top each with a chocolate kiss.

(An alternative is to use the refrigerated rolled peanut butter cookie dough, cut into quarters, put into mini-muffin pans and bake. Add kiss on top while dough is warm. Cool well before serving.)

247

## Ladybug Cookies
### (kids will go buggy for these!)

*2 dozen*

24 vanilla wafers

24 chocolate sandwich cookies

1 tube red cake decorating icing

1 6-ounce package semi-sweet chocolate chips

24 chocolate kisses

Spread red cake icing on vanilla wafers. Cut wafers in half. Place red wafers as wings on top of sandwich cookies, using icing to attach them. Place chocolate chips on the wings for the spots. Attach chocolate kiss in position as the ladybug's head.

They look so silly that the kids will love them.

## Peanutty Cornflake Treat

*Makes 24*

1 cup light corn syrup

1 cup sugar

1 cup extra crunchy peanut butter

6 cups cornflakes

In medium saucepan combine corn syrup and sugar. Bring to a boil and stir until sugar is dissolved. Remove from heat and add peanut butter. Stir well. Pour mixture over 6 cups cornflakes and mix. Drop by tablespoons onto wax paper.

## Greatest Chocolate Chip Cookies

*4 to 5 dozen*

1 cup butter or margarine

1 cup peanut butter, crunchy works best

1 cup sugar

1 cup brown sugar

2 eggs

1 teaspoon vanilla

2 cups flour

1 teaspoon baking soda

1 12-ounce package miniature chocolate chips,
   may use regular size

Preheat oven to 325°F. Cream together butter and peanut
butter. Add sugar, brown sugar, eggs and vanilla. Mix well.
Add flour and soda, mixing well. Fold in chocolate chips.
Drop a tablespoon of dough onto a greased cookie sheet.
Bake 15 minutes. Let cookies cool a few minutes prior to
removing from cookie sheet.

 **Idea!**
Using fun-shaped cookie cutters help bring
sandwiches to life!

249

### Lemonade Cake
*10 to 15 servings*

1 6-ounce can frozen lemonade concentrate

1/2 to 3/4 cup sugar

1 lemon cake mix

4 eggs

1 small package lemon instant pudding

3/4 cup water

3/4 cup salad oil

Preheat oven to 350°F. Mix lemonade concentrate with sugar and let stand while mixing cake. Combine cake mix, eggs, lemon instant pudding, water and oil. Pour into well greased and floured tube pan. Bake 1 hour. When cake is taken from oven, spoon lemonade and sugar mixture over the top and let stand for 1 hour in pan.

This is a great cake for picnics or cook-outs, no icing and it stays so moist.

### Tutti-Frutti Cones
*4 servings*

1 cup fresh fruit, such as strawberries or blueberries

1/4 cup sugar

2 8-ounce cartons flavored yogurt

4 ice cream cones

Combine fruit, sugar and yogurt in blender, blend until smooth. Pour mixture into a small container and cover with plastic wrap or lid. Freeze for 12 hours. Scoop out the frozen yogurt and serve in ice cream cones.

## Elephant's Delightful Edibles

*12 to 16 servings*

14 tablespoons butter, softened

1 cup graham cracker crumbs

1 16-ounce box powdered sugar

1 cup creamy peanut butter

1 6-ounce package semi-sweet chocolate chips

Combine butter and graham cracker crumbs. Stir in powdered sugar and peanut butter. Press into an 8 x 8-inch pan.

Melt chocolate chips and spread over mixture. Place in the refrigerator for chocolate to cool, 10 to 15 minutes.

Cut into squares and return to refrigerator until completely cooled.

## Wacky White Chocolate Crunchies

**(Keep away from the grown-ups!)**

*Makes 12 to 14 cups*

1 pound white chocolate

3 cups rice square cereal

3 cups corn square cereal

3 cups toasted oat cereal

2 cups stick pretzels

2 cups dry roasted peanuts

1 12-ounce package of candy coated chocolates

Melt white chocolate in top of double boiler over simmering water. Combine all other ingredients. Slowly pour chocolate over mixture and stir to evenly coat. Spread the mixture on wax paper and let cool. Break into small pieces. Store in airtight container and refrigerate to keep fresh.

### Let's Eat the Play Dough

1/3 cup margarine

1/3 cup light corn syrup

1/2 teaspoon salt

1 teaspoon vanilla

16 ounce box of powdered sugar

5-6 drops of food coloring

Place all the ingredients in the bowl and mix well.

Fun to play and eat. Great for decorating cookies too! It is yummy in your tummy!

### Yummy Gummy Mix

**Makes 5 cups**

1 cup gummy bears

1 cup candy corn

1 cup raisins, any type

1 cup miniature marshmallows

1 cup pretzel twists

Place all ingredients in mixing bowl, toss together and serve.

Variations: Add holiday candy to go with the season, or for older kids add peanuts.

## Buggies in a Ruggie

*50 to 60 bite-size pieces*

8 ounces reduced fat cream cheese, softened

1/3 cup powdered sugar

3/4 teaspoon cinnamon

1/2 teaspoon vanilla extract

1/4 cup raisins

6 flour tortillas

Combine cream cheese, powdered sugar, cinnamon and vanilla extract until smooth. Stir in raisins. Spread three tablespoons of mixture evenly over tortilla shells, roll, and twist ends to seal. Wrap each one separately in plastic wrap.

Refrigerate until chilled. Slice into 1/2 inch pieces.

## Cheetas Bananas

Any number of bananas, peeled and sliced in half

Chocolate hard coat topping

Popsicle sticks

Sprinkles

Spread wax paper on a cookie sheet. Peel bananas, cut in half. Insert popsicle stick in banana. Hold banana over another pan and pour chocolate topping or roll in sauce. Top with sprinkles. Place on wax paper and freeze until hard. Place in individual plastic bags. Frozen fun treats!

## Gator Blue and Oranges

*makes 10 orange halves*

2   3-ounce packages of blue gelatin

1 1/2 cups boiling water

2 cups cold water

5 oranges, sliced in half, pulp removed

1 can of whipped cream

candy sprinkles

Dissolve gelatin in boiling water, stirring constantly. Stir in 2 cups cold water. Place scooped out oranges in muffin tins to keep them from falling over.

Fill orange "bowls" with blue gelatin to the top. Chill until firm. Serve with a dot of whipped cream on top and candy sprinkles if desired.

## Monkey Bread for Munchkin's Makin'

4 10-count cans refrigerated biscuits

1 cup sugar

5 tablespoons cinnamon

1 cup of melted margarine or butter

Preheat oven to 350°F. Grease a bundt pan. Cut biscuits into quarters. Combine sugar and cinnamon in a large resealable plastic bag. Drop biscuits a few at a time into bag and shake to coat thoroughly. (Fun for children) Pour any left over cinnamon-sugar over biscuits. Pour melted butter over the top and bake 15 to 20 minutes.

Turn bundt pan over onto cake plate. Delicious served warm.

## Dream Cookies
(Dream up your own design)

*size of the cookie cutter determines the yield*

1   3-ounce package cream cheese. softened

1 cup butter or margarine. softened. not melted

1 egg yolk

1 cup granulated sugar

1/2 teaspoon vanilla extract

2 1/2 cups all-purpose flour

Preheat oven to 350°F. Cream together the cream cheese and butter. Add egg yolk and sugar: mix well. Stir in vanilla. Gradually sift in the flour until thoroughly mixed. Divide dough in half: wrap each half in plastic wrap. Chill dough 20 to 30 minutes.

Working with half of chilled dough at a time. roll dough to 1/8 or 1/4-inch thick. on a lightly floured surface.

Use cookie cutters to cut out cookies. Place cookies on ungreased cookie sheet. Bake 10 to 12 minutes. until light golden brown.

## Jiggly-Wiggly Chocolate Bites
(These are very rich and you can add whipped cream topping if you wish)

*makes 16 bites*

4  1-ounce envelopes of unflavored gelatin

1   12-ounce package of chocolate chips

1/2 cup sugar

1 1/2 cups cold water

Combine all ingredients in medium saucepan. cook over low heat 5 minutes or until chocolate is melted. Pour into 9-inch square pan. Chill in refrigerator until firm. Cut into 1-inch squares or smaller. What a treat!

### Children's Choice Menu

It's a big decision— what to have for dinner.

Make your children feel extra special by letting them help plan a menu. They will also enjoy the time you spend together preparing it. Have fun with the favorites listed below. which were given an A+ by young taste testers.

Cornflake
Chicken Strips
page 240

More Macaroni
and Cheese.
If You Please
page 241

Cabana
Banana Slaw
page 243

Pirate's
Corn Delight
page 245

Flippin' Fruit Smoothies
page 246

Chocolate
Noodle Nests
page 256

Monster Cookies
page 257

Gerald H. McCoy,
Jr., CPA, PA

255

## Chocolate Noodle Nests

*Makes approximately 30 depending on size*

1 12-ounce package semi-sweet chocolate morsels

1 12-ounce package butterscotch morsels

2 cups chow mein noodles

1/2 teaspoon vanilla extract

1 cup jelly beans

Melt chocolate and butterscotch in saucepan over low heat. Add noodles and vanilla. Drop by teaspoons on waxed paper. Top "nests" with several jelly bean "eggs". Allow to cool.

This recipe was "Graciously" tested and named by Mrs. Hatcher's 1st grade class at Martha Manson Academy.

256

### idea!

Lightly press fun-shaped cookie cutters into the icing of cupcakes. Pipe colored icing along the outlines.

## MONSTER COOKIES
*makes 18 cookies*

1 cup shortening or oil

1 cup sugar

1 cup brown sugar

2 eggs

1 1/2 cups flour

1 teaspoon soda

1 teaspoon salt

3 cups quick oats

1 teaspoon vanilla

1 12-ounce package semi-sweet chocolate chips

walnuts, optional

Preheat oven to 375°F. Melt shortening in saucepan. Add sugar, brown sugar and eggs; mix well. Stir in flour, soda, salt, oats, vanilla, chocolate chips and nuts. Drop by tablespoon onto ungreased cookie sheet. Bake 7 to 10 minutes until brown.

 **idea!**
Pour cake batter into flat-bottomed ice cream cones to half full. Bake as directed by cake recipe. Decorate with icing and fun-colored sugars.

## Fun Finger Paint

3 tablespoons sugar

1/2 cup cornstarch

2 cups cold water

Powdered tempera paint

Mix sugar, cornstarch and water together. Cook over low heat until thick, stirring constantly. Cool and pour into a muffin tin adding a different color to each one.

## Feed the Birds

1 large open pine cone

1/2 cup peanut butter

1 cup bird seed

Spread the peanut butter all over the pinecone. Then roll the pinecone in the bird seed until it is completely covered.

Tie a piece of yarn around the top to hang it. Hang in your yard, watch out for incoming birds.

Contributors

## PLATINUM SPOONS

AvMed Health Plan

Clark & Deborah Butler-Butler Plaza, The Miracle Mile;
Sarah and Reed Brown;
Eric W. Scott, MD, dba Florida Neurosurgical Associates

ComQuest Designs, Inc.

Eric W. Scott, MD
dba Florida Neurosurgical Associates

Kitchen & Spice and other things nice

The Junior League of Gainesville Past Presidents

Shands HealthCare

The Village Retirement Center

Without your support, our color pages would not exist.
Thank you!

## GOLD SPOONS

Abby Fromang Milon,
  Attorney at Law
Ameriprint
Brittany's Fine Jewelry
Clayton & Bzoch, Builders
  of Fine Homes
Country Cobbler
Dr. & Mrs. Thomas M. Brill
Florida Food Service
Gainesville Family
  Physicians
Gerald H. McCoy Jr.,
  CPA, PA
Holbrook Travel, Inc.
James D. Salter, Esquire
James Moore & Co., CPAs
John Petrich, Northwestern
  Mutual Life
Katy Graves
Lentz Financial Group

Meadowbrook Golf
  Course
Richard W. Oliver Jr.,
  DMD, PA
Robbins Eye Clinic
Robinshore, Inc.
Sam N. Holloway
  & Co., Inc.
Sovereign Restaurant
Spa King
Steve's Café
  Americain, Inc.
Sweetwater Branch Inn
The Junior League of
  Gainesville 1996-97
  and 1997-98
  Executive Committees
The Junior League of
  Gainesville 1996-97
  Provisional Class
Waldo's Antique Village

 SILVER SPOONS

A Storage Center
Barbara R. Menzies
Brown and Cullen, Inc.
Carla Brice
Carolyn G. Pooley
Central Florida Tile
  & Marble Co.
Charles D. Sapp, PE & RLS
Darla Raines
Doris Horton-Career
  Connections
Dr. and Mrs. Melvin C. Dace
Emerson Appraisal
First American Title
  Insurance Company
Gainesville State Bank
Grace N. Franklin
Laura T. Carmichael

J.J. Luckey & Co., CPAs
Jody & Suellen Davis
Madeline H. Chance
Mr. & Mrs. Howard Hall
Marian C. Ryland
Mr. & Mrs. James E.
  Sproull, Jr.
Mr. & Mrs. Sidney
  Bowdoin
Mrs. D.R. Matthews
Mrs. William D. Frederick
Robert M. Fox, DMD
SunTrust Bank,
  North Central Florida
Tyler, Troy and Trace
  Rucarean
U.S. Title
Virginia & Megan Guyton

261

The Cookbook Committee is indebted to the following Junior League members and friends in the community who unselfishly gave time and talent to this project. *Gracious Gator Cooks* would not be a reality without their contributions of recipes, testing of recipes, typing, proofreading, editing, consulting and more.

| | | |
|---|---|---|
| Barbara Agee | Annie Bzoch | Paul Dwyer |
| June Allen | Sara Campen | Rhonda Edelstein |
| Irma Alvarez | Kathy Cannon | Ann Emerson |
| Joe Anderson | Laura Carmichael | Martha Emerson |
| Joseph Gaa Anderson | Susan Black Carter | Danielle Enneking |
| Kim Anderson | Teresa Caskey | Randy Everett |
| Dodie Andrews | Luann Cawlfield | D. A. Fosser |
| Maritza Arroyo | Mary Cawlfield | Carrie Fagan |
| Lee Avera | Madeline Chance | Alice Farkash |
| Marge Baker | Ramona Chance | Barbara Feather |
| Ryan Baptiste | Toni Chatman | Cathy Feathers |
| Lorraine Barber | Debbie Christiansen | Cherie Fine |
| Patti Bartlett | Dana Clayton | Dawn Flanegan |
| Laura Batlle | Marian Close | Deirdre Fogler |
| Anna Bell | Jean Clough | Gale Ford |
| Garrett Bell | Julie Cofren | Amy Fouts |
| Marty Bell | Ann Coker | Carolyn Fouts |
| Vivian Bender-Walker | Caroline Coleman | Rosy Fox |
| Cathy Bishop | Cindy Comfort | Melba Fuller |
| Rita Boling | Margo Cook | Mary Ellen |
| Tara Boonstra | Stephanie Coon | Funderburk |
| Kerry Borer | Rhonda Copley | Elizabeth Furlow |
| Leslie Bovay | Andrea Cornelius | Jean Gadd |
| Angie Bowdoin | Kathy Counts | Pat Gager |
| Nancy Brandi | Beth Davis | Stacy Garnett |
| Judy Brashear | Helen Davis | Melanie Gasper |
| Dorothy Briggs | Stephanie Davis | Wanda Gay |
| Joan Brock | Margie Deardourff | Lisa Gearen |
| Kimberly Brock | Terrie DeFord | Vicki Gehman |
| Pete Brown | Nannette Dell | Nelda George |
| Dorothy Brunet | Charles H. Denny, III | Lucille George |
| Joel Buchanan | Wanda Denny | Melissa Glikes |
| Rie Burton | Maggie Downey | Carol Glover |

| | |
|---|---|
| Charlene Godley | Kathy Joyner |
| Karen Godley | Liza Kephart |
| Kathy Grantham | April Kirch |
| Katy Graves | Kelley Kirk |
| Ellen Gray | Susan Kirkland |
| Pamela Green | Ellen Kirkpatrick |
| Rhonda Green | Dawn Kraft |
| Mackey Gremillion | Melanie Kretzman |
| Kitty Griffin | Kirby Kriz |
| Pam Griskel | Caroline Lane |
| Laura Gruber | Mark Lawrence |
| Shea Grundy | Valentine Lee |
| Barbara Guyton | Cathy Lentz |
| Carol Hadley | Emily Lentz |
| Pamela Haines | Franklin K. Lentz, Jr. |
| Ellen Hall | Maura Lewis |
| Rosalind Hall | Jan Everett Lindner |
| Donna Hankin | Judy Locascio |
| Elizabeth Hawker | Patty Locascio |
| Amy Lewallen Hartley | Paul Locascio |
| Nancy Henry | Dr. Catherine Longstreth |
| The Heritage Club | Jean Lore |
| Cornelia Holbrook | Louise Lowe |
| Charise Holcomb | Anita Lowry |
| Carrie Holloway | Aggie Magula |
| Connie Holloway | Diane Mahaffey |
| Cynthia Holt | Pat Mann |
| Doris Horton | Denise Mansheim |
| Gretchen Howard | Wes Marston |
| Leigh Ann Howe | Nancy Mason |
| Teri Howell | Sara Matthews |
| Linda Ireland | Martha Loggins |
| Nan Islam | McClammy |
| Margaret Jarrell-Cole | Robin McClanathan |
| Catherine Jenkins | Melinda McCoy |
| Recie Jenkins | Amy McGee |
| Jackie Johnson | Yvette McIntyre |
| Jody Jones | Beth McKenzie |

Evelyn McKnight
Sally McKinley
Susan McKinney
Kim McMullan
Barbara Menzies
LouAnn Messina
Marie F. Miller
Beth Mills
Karen Morey
Lori Moshyedi
Kim Mueller
Ellen Mullarkey
Courtney Muse
Becker Myers
Cathy Nell
Linda Newman
Vivian Nolan
Emily O'Hara
Ricky Oliver
Truitt Oliver
Frances Pappas
Adelaide Parker
Mary Katherine
  Parker
Mary Parrish
Polly Pepper
Pamela Perry
Vicki Peters
Rainer Pinkoson
Father David Pittman
Carolyn Pooley
Jo Ann Porter
Laura Press
Mary Press
Frank Procter
Fay Prost
Connie Quincey
Darla Raines
Elizabeth Ray

Marla Reece
Belinda Rembert
Marianne Robbins
Jeanne Rochford
Sue Rohrlack
David Rovell-Rixx
Helen Rucarean
Linda Sue Rucarean
Helen Sabis
Eleanor Samuels
Nancy Sanders
Suzanne Sawyer
Melanie Shore
  Schackow
Lynn Schackow
Julie Scheck
Kerry Schmidt
Connie Schott
Larry Schott
Jenny Scott
Robin Scott
K.K. Serrins
Delle Sieg
Ilene Silverman-Budd
Christine Smith
Derek Smith
Iva Smith
Jane Smith
Kari Smith
Kathy Smith
Millie Smith
Rick D. Smith
Karen Smittle
Robin Snyder
Neeta Someshwar
Linda Sproull
Eva Squires
Ginger Stegall
Emily Stringer

Mary Stringfellow
Robbie Stringfellow
Maggie Stryker
Tracy Stubbs
Debbie Sun
Kim Teegen
Dorie Thomas
Karen Thomas
Sally Thompson
Caroline Thurber
Sara Torbert
Cindy Townsend
Stephanie Turner
Mindy Underberger
Andrea Valdyke-Tootle
Carol Villemaire
Anne Wallace
Helen Wallace
John Walsh
Mary Walsh
Suzanne Warner
Margaret Watts
Jodi Webb
Annette Wilbert
Eve Wilder
Frances B. Williams
Sarah Williams
Steve Williams
Peggy Williams
Terry Wilson
Julianne Witt
Elaine Wright
Allison Zant
Margaret Zeanah
Carole Zegel

# Index

265

267

### GRACIOUS
### Gator Cooks

*from the Junior League of Gainesville, Florida, Inc.*

Please send _____ copies of *Gracious Gator Cooks* @ $19.95 each   $ _____

Florida residents add appropriate sales tax                         $ _____

Shipping and Handling                                     $ _____

    ($3.50 each book; subject to sales tax for Florida residents)    **Total**   $ _____

Ship To:

Name: _____

Address: _____

City: _____ State: _____ Zip Code: _____

Method of Payment    _____ Check   _____ Credit Card

*Please make checks payable to the Junior League of Gainesville, Florida, Inc.*

P.O. Box 970 · Gainesville, FL 32602

Visa/Mastercard Number: _____

Card Holder Name: _____

Expiration Date _____

Signature _____

Credit Card Orders may be placed by calling (352) 376-3805 or fax (352) 371-4994

*Proceeds from the sale of this book support the projects of the Junior League of Gainesville, Florida, Inc.*

— — — — — — — — — — — — — — — — — — — — — — — — —

### GRACIOUS
### Gator Cooks

*from the Junior League of Gainesville, Florida, Inc.*

Please send _____ copies of *Gracious Gator Cooks* @ $19.95 each   $ _____

Florida residents add appropriate sales tax                         $ _____

Shipping and Handling                                     $ _____

    ($3.50 each book; subject to sales tax for Florida residents)    **Total**   $ _____

Ship To:

Name: _____

Address: _____

City: _____ State: _____ Zip Code: _____

Method of Payment    _____ Check   _____ Credit Card

*Please make checks payable to the Junior League of Gainesville, Florida, Inc.*

P.O. Box 970 · Gainesville, FL 32602

Visa/Mastercard Number: _____

Card Holder Name: _____

Expiration Date _____

Signature _____

Credit Card Orders may be placed by calling (352) 376-3805 or fax (352) 371-4994

*Proceeds from the sale of this book support the projects of the Junior League of Gainesville, Florida, Inc.*